The Money Revolution

The Money Revolution

*Easy ways to manage your finances
in a digital world*

Anne Boden

KoganPage

First published in Great Britain and the United States in 2019 by Kogan Page Limited

2nd Floor, 45 Gee Street
London
EC1V 3RS
United Kingdom
www.koganpage.com

122 W 27th St, 10th Floor
New York, NY 10001
USA

4737/23 Ansari Road
Daryaganj
New Delhi 110002
India

© Starling Bank Limited, 2019

The right of Anne Boden to be identified as the author of this work has been asserted by her in accordance with the Copyright, Designs and Patents Act 1988.

ISBNs
Hardback   978 1 78966 062 3
Paperback   978 1 78966 061 6
eBook   978 1 78966 063 0

British Library Cataloguing-in-Publication Data
A CIP record for this book is available from the British Library.

Library of Congress Cataloging-in-Publication Data
Names: Boden, Anne (Banking entrepreneur), author.
Title: The money revolution : easy ways to manage your finances in a digital world / Anne Boden.
Description: 1st Edition. | New York : Kogan Page Ltd, [2019] | Includes bibliographical references and index.
Identifiers: LCCN 2019012421 (print) | LCCN 2019019390 (ebook) | ISBN 9781789660630 (Ebook) | ISBN 9781789660623 (hardback) | ISBN 9781789660616 (pbk.) | ISBN 9781789660630 (eISBN)
Subjects: LCSH: Finance, Personal. | Banks and banking–Technological innovations.
Classification: LCC HG179 (ebook) | LCC HG179 .B56683 2019 (print) | DDC 332.024–dc23

Typeset by Integra Software Services, Pondicherry
Print production managed by Jellyfish
Printed and bound by Ashford Colour Press Ltd

Contents

Acknowledgements

This book would never have been written without the help, support and knowledge of the exceptionally skilled team at Starling. I would like to thank each and every one of them. I would also like to acknowledge journalist Teena Lyons for assisting in getting the words onto the page and Greg Hawkins, our technical adviser, who read the book before it went to print and offered a number of hugely valuable observations.

I am also very grateful to Chris Cudmore and the team at Kogan Page who helped keep this book on track. Thank you also to Jeff Scott at Platypus PR for all his advice and to Starling's head of corporate affairs, Alexandra Frean, who made sure this book happened.

Introduction

There's no shortage of advice available when it comes to the money in our wallets. There are apparently countless ways to save more effectively, or get better returns on investments, or to pay back debts quicker. Some of it is useful, a lot of it is confusing and, worst of all, it is very easy to ignore altogether if you really would rather not think about it at all for now.

This book turns it all around. *The Money Revolution* is a simple guide to everything you need to know about the new, easy and transparent way to get control of your finances.

Thanks to technology, it is now possible to effortlessly know exactly what you have to save, spend and invest, down to the last penny or cent, now and for months and years to come. Our smartphones offer a dizzying array of possibilities to help keep track of our money, make it work harder and budgeting a breeze. If you want to know how to save money without even noticing it, or smoothly keep track of investments, or simply view all your incomings and outgoings in one place, there are dozens and dozens of apps for that. It doesn't matter if you are someone who has always been in the red, or if you don't even know what being in the red means: it's great to know exactly where it is all going, so you can adjust course and keep everything in check if you need to.

The Money Revolution is divided into two parts. The first part gives a broad overview of all the latest developments in banking and finance and a snapshot of what you might expect in the near future. The second takes each aspect of our financial lives in turn, be it savings, mortgages, pensions or insurance, and describes the best apps currently available in the UK and around the world. There is no compulsion to read it in chronological order. You may like to dive right in, download some apps and start improving your money management right away. That's absolutely fine: the choice is yours. You will find that all of the apps featured here are designed to be simple to use and easy to understand: no previous tech experience is required. This book is written along the same lines. I want you to get the best out of your money and hope to show you some fantastic tools with which to do it.

If you've ever made a silent vow to get your finances in order, this book will set you in the right direction.

PART ONE

Busting the money myths

CHAPTER ONE

Take control of your money

You are in charge

Transform the way you use money

Developments in smartphone and data sharing technology are transforming how we save, spend and invest our money. Our interactions with the world around us are now completely different thanks to sensors, cloud computing and WiFi, which surround us everywhere we go. With our every individual move noted and logged, it has become possible for us to be charged only for the actual *time* that we use particular services. To the second. Forget about dull, predictable monthly bills that have to be paid regardless of how much or how little you use a service: pay-as-you-go is set to become the new norm.

This book is a guide to some of the latest products and services that can and will transform the way you view and use your money. Thanks to a wave of new banking, savings, investment and pension apps it is now possible to understand more about your money and take control of it in a way you have simply never been able to do in the past. And don't worry, you don't have to be a tech genius or a money markets expert to understand it all. That's the point. Most of the time all you will need is a smartphone and the will to make your cash work a bit harder for you.

You don't have to be a tech genius or a money markets expert. All you need is a smartphone and the will to make your cash work harder.

You can, if you like, think of it as outwitting the established global finance industry that has previously thrived on the status quo where no one really understood what was happening with their hard-earned cash. This book will show you the most up-to-date financial tools available and how they simplify what happens with money, creating a more even playing field. I can even show you how to make money out of your banks, instead of them always making money from you. Yes, we are talking about the complete reinvention of the inefficient, over compensated, financial business model.

It's not that any reasonable person begrudges banks and financial institutions making money. They are, after all, businesses, and if they don't make money, they wouldn't be able to survive. No, it is the sheer amount of cash that many of the big firms make from their customers that has made many ordinary people baulk. Worse still, no one is ever really sure how they do it. In the past, finance has been one of the least transparent services available, and you'd be forgiven for thinking that this is just how some of the large institutions like it. You don't need to scratch too far below the surface to find a breath-taking range of ways that they eat into your hard-earned cash. Free bank account? Not really. They make up the shortfall with inflated charges on interest and unauthorized overdrafts. Great loan deal? Maybe, but how much did you pay in fees? Going abroad?

Check your statement when you get home because all those trips to international ATMs add up in ways you'd never have anticipated.

The problem is, unless you are the type of person who always watches your bank balances, insurance premiums and pension contributions like a hawk and are on top of every single transaction, it's not that easy to work out where it all goes. Payments are not always transparent, and fees on transactions are either hugely complex or neatly hidden away. Even if you are especially careful, there has frequently been no real way of getting to the bottom of what you are paying for in a service. It doesn't help that the smoke and mirror show around our cash is built on a foundation of myths about our money and what happens to it. These myths promote 'truths' such as that banks can always be trusted to have your best interests at heart, or that independent advisers are truly independent, even though these beliefs have been disproved time and again (often in the most dramatic and ruinous ways). Meanwhile, glossy ads for any sort of financial services organization declare their customer friendly credentials, yet it has often been difficult to get any sort of coherent explanation about the products they back. Any information dispensed by the institutions that are supposedly championing our financial cause frequently feels very hard to come by too. Even so, the myths prevail and have helped to keep many people in the dark about their finances ever since they became adults and started earning a wage. The persistence of these uncertainties frequently makes anything to do with saving, spending and investing feel like a leap in the dark.

No one needs to put up with this confusion over money today. Banking, and indeed anything to do with managing our finances, has been undergoing a radical makeover. In fact, it would not be overstating it to say we're going through the biggest and most rapid shift in our relationship with money for hundreds of years. Perhaps ever. It's a money revolution. Thanks to advances in technology, from machine learning, to artificial intelligence (AI), to robo-advising, there are widespread opportunities to not just understand more about where your money is going but also to take complete charge of it and make it work better for you.

Why this book now?

My credentials for writing this book are born out of working in banking and finance for my whole career. I have worked on both 'sides': initially within so-called traditional banks where the model has barely changed for decades. I now head one of the most successful of the new breed of highly entrepreneurial fintechs (an abbreviation of financial and technology) that have turned on its head the way we think about and use money.

My first job was as a graduate trainee at Lloyds Bank, and I worked my way up through executive positions at Standard Chartered Bank and UBS before moving to head global transaction banking across 34 countries for ABN Amro and RBS. My final position, before I decided it was time to do things differently, was as chief operating officer of Allied Irish Bank (AIB). I was headhunted there with a brief to turn around the then debt-ridden bank that had been taken over by the Irish government in the wake of the global financial crisis that hit in 2007–08. Although the Irish bank was returned to profitability, the experience had a big impact on me. Radically cutting costs while tens of thousands of Irish citizens suffered the ongoing effects of the financial crisis made me question whether we were approaching things in the right way at all. It became glaringly obvious that there was something very wrong with existing banking practices. While everyone else in my sector was desperately trying to reinstate the exact same model of the established business of finance that had been ripped apart by the global credit crunch and subsequent government bailouts, it was all underpinned by cumbersome, legacy systems and inbuilt bureaucracy that had arguably contributed to the problem in the first place. Surely this was the very time we should all be doing some soul searching and looking at doing things an entirely different way? With no one else in my industry seemingly interested or willing to do this, I decided to take on the task myself.

After taking some time out to analyse the way financial systems worked, which was a process that took me around the world on a fact-finding mission, I formed a vision for a new digital bank that would use the latest technology to genuinely put the customer first and give them ever greater choice. My new bank would have no physical branches because it would operate from the smartphones we all have with us all day, every day, making my money services accessible 24/7. The philosophy of this service would not be predicated on a mission to *sell* customers products. It would be a service that looked after customers and catered to their needs, rather than the other way around. As I developed my idea, I realized I was at the beginning of an opportunity to fundamentally change our relationship with finances, just as Amazon had changed shopping and iTunes had changed music.

Starling, the mobile bank I created in 2014, has gone on to become one of modern banking's biggest success stories, winning multiple awards and, of course, hundreds of thousands of new customers. After starting life as the UK's first mobile-only current account, Starling now offers business accounts, joint accounts and a marketplace offering a range of partnerships with complementary financial partners from mortgage brokers to pensions providers. Each of the partners is carefully checked to ensure it matches the bank's philosophy of being accessible, transparent and easy to use. Most importantly, it has to put the customer in charge of their own finances.

The challenge of traditional banks

One of the things I have most enjoyed about working with developers that I have met through our marketplace and the fintech community, is the 'can do' attitude that I frequently encounter. In my previous life, working for bricks-and-mortar banks, the tendency was to accept things as they were because it had always been done that way. Often, even if there was an inkling that it could be done better or in a more convenient way for customers, no one did anything because someone, somewhere said it couldn't be done. Discussion closed.

One of my most memorable examples of this occurred when I was at AIB. As well as working on rebuilding trust with our fed-up customer base, the bank was keen to build up its current account business, which meant attracting new customers. It seemed to me that the most obvious pinch point to tackle in this objective was the lengthy (and extremely off-putting) processes that needed to be ticked off before an account was declared open and a customer received their debit cards. 'It needs to be vastly simplified,' I said.

In my view it was no wonder that people would doggedly stick with their chosen bank for an average of 17 years, a feat of apparent extreme loyalty that even surpasses that displayed in most British marriages that last on average just 11 years and 6 months. At that time, it wasn't as if any of the other high street banks were even offering a fantastic, top notch service that made it almost impossible to leave for pastures new. In fact, frequently quite the opposite was true. Most banks offered more or less identical products and services. It was easy to assume that no one wanted to change out of sheer lethargy, but it was equally likely that even if they were entirely fed up with their existing bank, they were put off switching by the complex and slow application process. (At that time there was also an element of concern over the potential risk of direct debits or crucial payments going astray, but that was resolved when the automatic transfer of incoming and outgoing payments when switching bank was introduced in the UK in September 2013.)

The reaction to my proposal to speed things up with a vastly simplified account opening process was instant. 'That's not going to happen,' I was told by a senior colleague.

Of course, I pressed the issue. I needed to know *why* customers needed to jump through multiple hoops to open an account. The basis for any new business drive is surely to make one proposition vastly more attractive than another. The only way I could convince you to change your bank would be to make it as quick and painless as possible, right?

The more I pushed, the more reasons I found it couldn't be done. It was due to 'compliance' or 'central bank rules', or any number of other reasons that didn't seem to make sense. Determined to get to the bottom of it, I delved into the answers I'd been given, trying to discover which rule was actually correct. With so many differing reasons, one had to be right. It was simply a question of finding it, and then I could work out if there was a way to get it changed or certainly to request it was made more appropriate to current practices. Do you know what? Many of the rules I had been quoted didn't exist at all. My banking colleagues were all hugely bright people, but a lot of what they believed was what they had been told by their predecessors. It was the worst case of Chinese whispers I had ever come across. Statements had been passed down through generation after generation of bankers with not one question asked because it was 'the rule you had to follow'. Meanwhile, you, the customer, shrugged your shoulders and stuck with what you had, because (a) the alternative was just the same, and (b) changing was a pointless hassle.

Challenging the myths of traditional finance

My awakening to the mythology around account-opening prompted me to start to look into all the other 'certainties' in banking and finances. The stuff we all accepted because it was forever thus. Was it possible we were all bumping along believing one thing, when nothing could be further from the case? I wondered just how many things we were tacitly accepting as they were because they were always that way.

My research led me to the question of high street bank branches. As everyone knows, bank branches have been closing in every district, and there is a high probability that you have seen several banks disappear in your area over the past decade or so. In the UK alone, bank branches have been shuttered at an average rate of 300 a year since 1989, but the trend has accelerated over recent years as big banks respond to pressure on profits by cutting costly bricks-and-mortar outlets. It is an emotive subject with many local communities becoming increasingly alarmed at the lack of provision in their area.

Once again, there are many myths and misconceptions about what is actually happening and why. The established line from banks is that branches are 'unprofitable'.

There are many myths and misconceptions about what is actually happening and why.

And that is, in fact, true. It is also true that most people barely use their local branches anymore. Many account holders don't visit *at all* from one year to the next. Many of the people who do still value physical banks, only do so because they wish to deposit change into their accounts: a practice banks have been actively discouraging for years.

What is most telling is what most major banks have chosen to do with their remaining estate, those branches they have decided to keep open to service areas with a large enough population to justify keeping them going. Of late, there has been a growing trend to bring all sorts of new digital gizmos into branches. If you've been into a bank branch recently, you may have noticed a proliferation of desktop screens that allow customers who attend a branch to speak to advisers directly, if remotely, via Skype or similar programmes. At my previous job with AIB, I was involved in one of the many initiatives to do this. We opened a very high-tech branch in Dundrum, Ireland, which was christened The Lab and billed as 'a new digital experience'. Even at the time I couldn't help but muse it had missed the point. Yes, customers clearly had an appetite for something a bit more high-tech, but what my bank and others were offering was a service that was not a whole lot different from what you could already get using your own PC in the warmth and comfort of your own home.

Interestingly though, Metro Bank, one of the new breed of retail banks, has turned the branch model on its head, with a great deal of success. It's introduced a very customer-friendly, open plan format, where banking staff are not hidden away behind thick screens but instead speak to customers on open counters. And, pride of place in every Metro Bank branch? A machine where customers can deposit change. Walk into any Metro Bank branch and you'll see these change counters in constant use. Why? It's what customers want.

The fact is that a bank is a business like any other. Banks should be moving with the times and courting its customers in the same way as any other sector of business. They should find out what customers want and give it to them. And, all the signs are that customers want more control over their own money.

Even today, after all the huge changes of the past few years, it still seems many banks are not listening. The various myths, with their level of confusion and misunderstanding about what customers can actually expect from banks, still exist. I have had several somewhat surprising conversations with potential customers in this respect.

'Will my bank get upset if I open another account?' asked one customer, who added for apparent clarification, 'I have been with them for ten years.'

Or:

'The bank will only *permit* one current account, right?'

We are, of course, allowed to have as many accounts as we choose and can chop and change within financial institutions to find the services that best suit our individual needs. Thanks to technological developments, this is easier than ever before too.

From a consumer point of view, it may feel like the system is still stacked against us. It's not just with banks either. Myths and confusion abound across the range of financial services. It's fairly certain that you have experienced an uneasy feeling over one or even several transactions you've made over the years, where you were not entirely sure where your money ended up, even if it was only for a few days. The lengthy time for cheque clearance has long been a bug bear, and actions like cross-border money transfers could see money taking up to three days to arrive at its destination even in a digital world. In pensions it is often hard to know what's what (and most importantly what to expect in retirement) unless you're a stickler for paperwork and, quite possibly, a whizz with a spreadsheet.

Anyone who has ever been charged a whopping fee for what seems like a relatively simple transaction would be forgiven for asking: why? The chances are though, even if they did pose the question, the answer would be fairly unclear. Historically, banks and financial institutions have been deliberately vague about the inner workings of the system. They are naturally resistant to the perceived threat to their dominance of the market if everything becomes so much more transparent. It could be they fear that if they try to alter the status quo or loosen their grip too much by updating and clarifying systems, the genie would be out of the bottle. Once people have the full picture, they will be free to compare and contrast. They'll also feel emboldened to explore all the incredible innovations that are occurring right now. As a result, the entire financial market could change and fragment, leading customers off on all sorts of exciting new paths. Nothing would ever be the same again.

Anyone who has ever been charged a whopping fee for what seems like a simple transaction would be forgiven for asking: why?

Why the future is fintech

Of course, the truth is, it is already happening. Over 50 per cent of customers globally are using at least one fintech firm to help manage their money, and 64 per cent of fintech users prefer using digital channels to manage all aspects of their financial lives.[1] The greatest take-up is in investment management (45 per cent), with 41 per cent adopting a new service for payments and transfers, 31 per cent for insurance and 29 per cent for banking.[2] Perhaps not surprisingly, younger, tech savvy and affluent consumers are leading the way, but the customer base is expanding all the time. What is certain is that the old, failing system, which was definitely biased towards the needs of big institutions, rather than consumers, is on the way out. Each new development offers measurable benefits to the everyday consumer.

The obvious question is: why don't large financial institutions ditch the cloak of respectability 'gained' by maintaining things as they have always been, with the customer kept firmly at arm's length? It could certainly be argued that they already have the advantage of the trust of consumers, or at least an established relationship with them anyhow. Surely, it would make sense for them to go with the flow and embrace the opportunity presented by the available new technology?

At present, there is no real sign of this happening. Most big banks and financial firms have adopted a wait-and-see mode, or have at best looked to forge relationships with fintech start-ups. Innovation won't come from the brands you have known all of your life. Many of the older, established financial institutions simply don't have technology that is advanced enough to keep up with the latest developments. Indeed, much of their infra-structure has roots going back three decades or more. Data capability is the domain of a new breed of fintechs, which have had the luxury of building their services from scratch with all the latest tech thinking.

This is why many of the companies that I mention in this book are in many cases only a few years old. These start-ups are unencumbered by legacy technology or legacy thinking. They are able to zoom in on and focus upon what is known in the industry as UX, or user experience. This means they have the capability to offer the very latest in digital thinking without worrying about how things used to be done. The sky really is the limit. They also have the luxury of being free to think out of the box when it comes to the user interface, or what your screen looks like when you log in and how you navigate around your accounts. Indeed, it is now increasingly common to be able to see balances in one place and transactions across all your financial accounts.

The new, more transparent financial system will, without a doubt, play a part in our individual attitudes to money. The current trend is all about putting control into the hands of individuals so they can make informed decisions. Again, it is a world away from the previous opaque order, where it was very easy for individuals to hide from potential issues with their finances. If you were the out-of-sight-out-of-mind type and preferred not to know about your balances, the system that most of us grew up with was all set up for it. Ignorance was bliss. Well, right up until it got so out of hand that both bank and customer were forced to react when, of course, it would have been easier to have got on top of it all in the first place. Likewise, if you are the type who often feels anxious or fearful about how much you have to your name, the lack of transparency can add to those negative emotions.

It's good to take responsibility for your own money

Like it or not, we can't put all the blame for any money woes onto banks and financial institutions. However complex it has been made for us in the past, we all have to take responsibility for our own finances. We all have deeply held beliefs about money that we have very little control over. Most of these thoughts stem from early childhood. One of my earliest memories was my father, Jack Boden, discussing some close neighbours who had joined the local golf club. Even though I was very young at the time, I easily picked up on his disapproval.

'We're never going to join the golf club,' he said categorically in a tone that

We all have deeply held beliefs about money that we have very little control over.

invited no debate. 'If we join the golf club we will be surrounded by people who spend more than us. It'll make us feel poorer.'

I know for a fact that this, and other similar things my parents said in passing, shaped my attitude to money. They still do, despite the fact I have worked in senior positions in financial environments for almost my entire working life and have therefore been subject to many, many different influences on my thinking. The way our parents handled money is the foundation for how we spend and save for the rest of our lives. Families who have little money but a spendthrift attitude about what they do have, will pass this on to their kids. Those who value wealth creation will generally impart their philosophies and strategies to the next generation.

It's not just the beliefs we've adopted from that early-years foundation that shape our attitude to money. We are also all subject to the significant influence that those around us have upon us, just as my father surmised. Think about it this way: if, for example, you get on a plane for your summer holiday flight and 'economy' is the only class of ticket available, then you'll barely give it a second thought. However, if you are flying economy but have to walk through the comfortable, spacious business class area on the way to your seat, it'll cast a shadow on the beginning of your getaway. All of a sudden you will feel a bit disgruntled about only being able to afford an economy ticket. These subtle influences have an impact on every walk of life, building upon our attitudes to money day by day. If your close friends get a super-sized, surround sound, cinema-style TV, it won't be long before you decide you have to have one. Got a mate with a passion for fast cars? The chances are, you'll be casting an eye over the motoring pages.

Don't worry, you are not alone in this. It's human nature. Whatever background you hail from, your emotions around money will be strong and hard to control. What we spend is connected to our feelings of self-worth. Many people are familiar with the experience of having their bank card refused, even if it is only a rare occurrence. When it happens, the most common reaction is one of deep shame. There is a real fear the cashier will think there is no money available in the account, regardless of the fact it could be due to a technical glitch or any number of other reasons. Separately, money has been blamed for relationship breakdowns, depression and even suicide. At the other end of the scale, an unexpected injection of cash from an inheritance or lottery win prompts feelings of elation or relief. These are all powerful emotions.

Obviously, the reality is that money *per se* is never the real problem or solution. If there are any issues with money, it is down to how we approach it, think about it and handle it day to day. It should go without saying that people who think negatively about money, or dislike thinking about it so much that they ignore it, are more likely to be plagued by financial problems. Whereas those who feel more relaxed about money and that it is in their control are more likely to be successful in any endeavour to increase the amount they own.

While it is an easy thing to say, but not such an easy thing to achieve, what we should be striving to develop is a healthier relationship with money.

The reason for bringing the subject up here is because it is not all one sided. Financial instructions are not solely to blame for our lack of control over our money: we also need to play a role in getting to grips with things. While we are being exposed to many fantastic new technological innovations right now, with many more just around the corner, they cannot be taken in isolation. The money revolution presents an opportunity to *rethink* our own individual attitudes to money and to unshackle ourselves from any previous negative connections in order to get the best from what is happening right now. Just as we have to adapt to an entirely new way of spending and saving, we can also completely reconsider our emotional connections to money that have been handed down from generation to generation.

Welcome to the money revolution

In my view, the new innovations in fintech put us into the perfect position to help us acclimatize. Take, as an example, mobile phone banking apps, which are my particular area of expertise. Mobile-only banks were not first to market with banking apps. Big banks produced app versions of their accounts before services like Starling were launched. However, I believe these early banking app versions from high street banks may have actually added to feelings of anxiety or shame about money, rather than assuaged them. The extremely basic early services showed the bare minimum of detail about a person's account, and there was little transparency around day-to-day spending, other accounts, savings or pensions. If anything, it was a shortened, less informative version of what account holders received every month via their paper statements. The new approach from digital banks is 180 degrees different. Starling Bank, for example, is built to be highly tactile. From facial recognition to ID your account, to detailed breakdowns of what you've spent on groceries, entertaining or household bills, it aims to promote a far more open relationship with money, making it a more visible, tangible, accessible experience. Nothing is hidden or mysterious. This opens up the potential for an attitudinal change to money and is a style that has been adopted by all the other mobile-only banks, such as Atom and Monzo. There is no limbo land of payments going in and disappearing for three days into the ether: everything is properly accounted for, so there are no surprises. Upcoming payments are even flagged in advance so account holders can make sure they have adequate funds ready. By getting rid of the unknowns and providing certainty for the longer term, the fears that fuel historic emotional connections will be vanquished.

The technology available now gives us the benefit of knowing down to the last penny what we have available to spend at any one time, whether it is one week from now, or one month, one year, or even to the end of our life. This development puts us in a very different position from that of previous generations. With the shackles of the traditional emotional connections with money broken, and the uncertainty removed, we are now free to look at our financial futures more objectively too. And, in my opinion, this has not come a moment too soon. The world is currently undergoing a seismic shift in how we live and work, with the rise of zero-hours contracts, fixed-term jobs and part-time work. It is crucial that we become more attuned to our finances if we want to successfully navigate these changes.

I suspect that many people reading this may be feeling a little wary. Any significant change is worrying, and we are in the midst of a money revolution that spells massive changes in the way we view and use money. There is certainly a lot to take in. Quite apart from how comfortable you feel with technological innovations, there is the question of the very strong emotions triggered by all things financial. It is understandable if there was a little bit of nostalgic hankering after that status quo, regardless of how misplaced so many of the myths were that underpinned it all.

Think in terms of taking control of your money and welcome the new era of openness and greater understanding.

My advice to anyone is to embrace what is happening as an entirely new way of doing things. Think in terms of taking control of your money and welcome the new era of openness and greater understanding. Embracing the money revolution and adopting a new attitude to money may well also lead onto a better acceptance of the changes to the wider world around us and the role we can play in it too.

To show you what I mean, let's look at housing. For generations buying a house has been seen as one of the most important investments that can ever be made. It has become the norm to invest in bricks and mortar to ensure a comfortable retirement and leave a respectable legacy to our families. With far, far less information at our fingertips than we have now, this often led to a situation where people either overshot, or under-did, their financial projections, with unfortunate consequences either way. Those who overshot would live extremely parsimoniously in order to purchase an expensive property and finish up leaving an enormous inheritance to their loved ones. While generous, this always seemed to me to be a bit of a waste. Everyone should be able to enjoy their life to the full and certainly not be scraping through in their best years. At the other end of the scale would be those who failed to keep enough put by to keep their homes through to an enjoyable old age, which then places a burden on the next generation. Neither scenario is good.

In many ways, trying to achieve the right balance of enjoying life and leaving a satisfactory legacy has been taken out of the hands of the current generation. These are the people who have become known as Generation Rent thanks to the lack of available housing to buy, low levels of council housing and soaring property prices, which have sparked a housing crisis. The private rented sector has grown enormously in recent years, accounting for nearly 4 million homes in the UK.

There has been a lot of hand-wringing coverage of what this will mean for the future, since people will no longer be saving hard for these big assets. What will we pass on to our heirs? I wonder though if this is looking at it from the wrong end of the telescope? There is surely no better reflection of the benefits of our gaining better control and understanding of what we have in the bank today, tomorrow and beyond. Ultimately, this better-informed generation now has the opportunity to live off less money and to make what money they do spend work as hard for them as it possibly can. Instead of planning around an arbitrary figure that will somehow accumulate in the months and years ahead, as our parents did (and not always terribly accurately at that), we can work towards a more manageable pay-as-you-go society.

A flexible approach to money

Renting flexibility fits in perfectly with the pay-as-you-go life-style we are now moving towards. Renters can live in a variety of areas, and if they don't like the neighbours or fancy travelling for a while, they can move when their contract comes to an end. Being in total control of your money means you can adopt an entirely different attitude from your forebears. Suddenly, being free of the long-term shackles of a mortgage doesn't sound so bad. That's even before you get to the freedom of not being responsible for the day-to-day maintenance of a property. If the boiler breaks or the roof tiles blow off, it is up to the house owner to fix it.

None of this is to advocate forgetting all long-term financial responsibilities. While pay-as-you-go is the new norm, we do all still need to think about our later years. I am constantly worried that many of the younger people I speak to nowadays are making no provisions whatsoever for their pensions. When I question them about it they say they have no idea of how to go about getting one, so they have decided to forget about it. Fortunately, the new way of tackling finances will play an enormous part in shifting the imbalance and will open the opportunity for people to take charge of their retirement planning. One of the most interesting fintech developments is automated advisers, also known as 'robo-advisers'. This represents a significant opportunity. A great deal of decision paralysis that stops pension investments comes down to general mistrust of financial advisers. This is not just down to a succession of well-publicized pensions mis-selling scandals either. No, many people find that financial advisers just don't always come across as credible or knowledgeable. There is a mistrust of what they say or their level of expertise. No one wants to entrust their financial future with someone who appears to be barely out of their training courses and who painstakingly follows a prescribed, box-ticking procedure. That does nothing to reassure people that they are getting a bespoke, tailored recommendation. Robo-advisers, on the other hand, offer an accessible, low-cost access to investments or, as it has been said, offer the same software as human advisers but at a considerably lower cost. They are more convenient too. Want pensions advice at 3 am? Then it is only a few taps away. Once again, it is all about choice. Your choice.

Robo-advisers are just one of many interesting developments that will change the way we view money, and I fully expect these innovations to have an impact on a wide range of financial decisions from simple financial planning, to investments, to pensions, to mortgages. Any recommendations will be backed by vastly improved analytics and data visualization that will give users a far clearer picture of their financial health. I will examine many individual applications throughout this book.

The important thing to remember is that consumers need no longer remain powerless bystanders when it comes to money. We are not being pushed along at the whim of the banks or even fintechs come to that, buffeted from one new idea to the next. We are being offered a plethora of quick, inexpensive ways to solve age-old problems to do with managing our money, which makes it easier to access it anytime, anywhere. We are in control though, and it is up to us which new developments we choose to take advantage of and when.

Most importantly, we are in the driving seat. We are not at the mercy of financial institutions and banks telling us what we need. We no longer need to take what we are given because there is nothing else on offer. Now that we have near ubiquitous access to high-power, low-cost computing and carry our technology with us wherever we go in the form of smartphones, we have high expectations and rightly so. Plus, after watching firms such as Apple and Amazon set the bar high in terms of the user experience, it is up to fintechs to impress us. If they want our business and loyalty, fintechs need to be at the top of their game. Constantly. No financial firm should ever take your business for granted ever again. And, if they do, you know what you can do: switch.

Whichever fintech firms succeed in leading the way in the new era for financial services, this way of doing business is a world apart from the 'us and them' situation of times gone by. Banks and financial institutions can no longer think in terms of capturing a customer and keeping them for life as they cross sell as many products as possible that suit the provider rather than the person paying the fees. To succeed in financial services, a provider needs to take a position as a genuinely 'trusted partner' and consistently offer the best products and services while providing consumers with all the tools to make a wise decision.

As customers, we are much, much better informed these days. This not only gives us more buying power but also puts us in a powerful position where, if we feel 'sold to' or manipulated towards something that blatantly doesn't suit our needs, we can go elsewhere. With much greater transparency around our finances, this is easier and easier to do. You and I are now more empowered than ever before to understand exactly what we are spending on a daily (even minute-by-minute) basis and to make a range of choices on that knowledge. It's time to make the most of it, and this book will show you how.

Notes

1   16best.net [accessed 22 January 2018] The incredible growth of fintech [Online] www.16best.net/blog/incredible-growth-fintech/
2   Capgemini (2017) *World FinTech Report 2017*, Capgemini, London

CHAPTER TWO

Be smart at building wealth

Join the uberization of cash revolution

Disruption arrives in the world of finance

If you are unfamiliar with the term disruptor, you definitely won't be unfamiliar with the firms that have driven the trend. Disruptors are organizations like Amazon, Airbnb and Uber. The once new-kids-on-the-block that came along, took over a previously established, cosy interface with the customer and then radically turned an entire industry on its head so nothing has ever been the same again. Now it is the turn of banks and finance firms, which are facing the biggest change to the way they do business for generations. This new shake up has been dubbed the uberization of money.

Disruption takes many forms, depending upon the industry. Sometimes, for example, disruptors bring us innovations that are completely new and yet entirely appropriate for the task in hand. It's hard to believe it now, but before Google (and other search engines) it was impossible to navigate the internet and find what you were looking for in seconds. Apple didn't invent the MP3 player, but their iTunes store innovation made it possible to instantly fill an iPod or iPhone with music. Other disruptive innovations have been based on making existing tasks a lot easier and accessible. If the disruptor gets it right, they can even create whole new markets. eBay is the perfect example of this. Before this online auction site came along, the only way for individuals to buy and sell items was through classified ads, at car boot sales or via specialist magazines. Obviously, that was a time-consuming and often inconvenient process, which is why a limited number of sellers were willing to give it a go. The founders of eBay correctly ascertained that a great deal of the magic about the internet was that small groups of interested parties could easily find one another for very little, if any, cost. It was the perfect forum to buy and sell goods privately. A couple of clicks and a deal could be done. eBay created a massive marketplace that lets millions of people participate with very little effort required. Scale and ease: the two priorities of any disruptor. Airbnb and Uber are in a similar position where they have taken an existing process and simplified it. They've taken the friction out of the process of renting a property or getting a taxi, and created new marketplaces.

What these disruptors all have in common is they have each targeted highly regulated industries and tackled them head on. Often, incumbent businesses have sought to halt the relentless progress of disruptors, and new laws have had to be created to fight or allow such services. In nearly every case, the powerful argument that these disruptors have used is that the regulations that governed their particular sector were created many years earlier for an entirely different era. They had since become overbearing, unnecessary and damaging to the best interests of customers.

Banking and disruption

Banking and finance is, arguably, the most highly regulated and well-scrutinized sector of them all, which is probably why it took a bit longer to get the full attention of disruptive forces. Despite the obvious existence of an un-served market, which would normally get the disruptors flocking, the scale of the challenge may just have seemed too great. For a real sign of just how difficult it has been perceived to be, consider the big four tech giants Amazon, Apple, Facebook and Google. According to some surveys, up to 40 per cent of customers of these four would welcome the ability to do their banking through these platforms.[1] However, none of the firms has rushed to get banking licences, although at the time of writing Apple has announced a credit card and Amazon is believed to be talking to US retail banks and has a range of payment tools.

The thinking seems to go that these large firms are perfectly placed to extend their reach still further into financial services. After all, they are already firmly in the sector, providing payment and other money-based services. The barriers to entry are not high if they wanted to increase their range. After all, like fintechs, they don't have the burden of an expensive branch and counter network that, say, high street banks do. Neither do they have the prohibitively high customer acquisition costs borne by most of the large firms in the financial services world. Amazon customers could just ask Alexa to take care of things when it comes to paying bills. Many commentators believe that these online giants are not going to aim to legally become banks in a traditional (and highly regulated) sense though. The closest they are expected to come to this is most likely to partner with existing banks, generating income through fees and royalties on an ever-widening range of products.

No, when it comes to big changes in this industry, the true innovations will not be led by established firms like the existing large financial institutions, or even the new breed of technology giants like Amazon. Just as in the case of other industries that have been turned on their heads, it is entirely new firms that have stolen a march and that will lead the way. In this sector it has been left to an innovative and growing group of fintech start-ups to come up with all the groundbreaking new stuff. In the same way as I looked at the 'all new' digital bank branches on the high street while working at AIB and thought there had to be a better way, so have other innovators looked at this aging financial industry and thought: hold on, why doesn't this work properly?

When it comes to big changes, the true innovations will not be led by established firms or even the new technology giants.

To remain with banking for a moment, it is important to say that disruption of the centuries-old banking model involves much more than just digitizing existing services. As with each of the disruptors that have gone before, it requires an entirely new way of thinking. When Starling Bank first started pondering how to create the bank of the future, the process went something along the lines of: banking isn't working, we need a completely different sort of bank, what do customers want and need? A handful of criteria stood out in particular:

- The customer needs a better, simpler, more accessible service that meets their needs and current lifestyle in a logical way.
- With an increasing number of financial products, banks and financial institutions, we need to play a role in demystifying everything that is on offer. Consumers need a large, transparent marketplace that brings together many buyers and sellers into the same virtual arena for a more convenient service.
- We need to put the customer's needs first (not the bank's), making every transaction cost effective, easy and hassle free, vastly improving the overall user experience.

- There are seemingly endless opportunities to make credit more accessible and available on better terms, to improve the process by which payments are made and received and, well, to just make the whole experience more inclusive.

The future is being mobile with money

Without a doubt, the future of financial services will centre around the smartphone: a device we all keep with us, all the time. That small piece of technology is slick, fast and convenient. There has already been a huge shift in consumer behaviour with respect to phone use and their money. Take banking as a starting point, since banks were among the first in the new generation of fintechs. While the early days of digital and telephone banking were largely confined to checking financial transactions via online accounts, we are now accustomed to using our phones for payments, transfers and much more. In fact, what we can do with our mobiles is evolving by the day. We can already do far more on our phones than in a physical bank branch, and at a better, more competitive price. It's much quicker too (and there are no queues).

The early days of digital and telephone banking were largely confined to checking financial transactions. Now we use our phones for so much more.

Mobile banks are, of course, not the only new disruptors to challenge the traditional finance industry. Thanks to the increased use of mobile phones and the advent of data services at affordable rates, numerous fintech firms are now looking at traditional financial services and working out how technology can make them work a lot better. There are new tech innovations in lending, mortgages, payment technology and pensions. In fact, practically every aspect of financial services is being disrupted.

The fintechs that are leading the way are characterized by a vision to create more value for the consumer with efficient, low-cost services that put customers at the centre of their operation. With each new app or service, customer expectations grow and the innovations flow.

The insurance industry is a sector that is currently at the early stages of the disruptive treatment, but there are already signs of some exciting developments. Take car insurance as a case in point. Until recently, most people have paid a (fairly significant) annual fee for the pleasure of owning and driving their car. If you own a car and are reading this now, it is more than likely that your vehicle is parked outside on the street or safely tucked away in a garage. In other words, you are not using it. In fact, unless you drive for a living, you probably won't use it for 90 per cent of the day. Some days you may not get behind the wheel at all. However, you are still paying to insure your vehicle. All day, every day. And, that's the galling part of car insurance: most people use their vehicle for a small fraction of the time yet have to pay large premiums that cover them 24/7.

Thanks to the latest developments in data technology, this scenario will soon become a thing of the past. Pay-as-you-go car insurance first appeared in 2017, doing away with the big upfront premium at a stroke. Users pay a flat monthly fee to cover the basic fire and theft element of the insurance policy, and then an extra charge on top each time they drive. If you don't drive, you don't pay. The process is all managed through a mobile phone app that logs each time a driver gets behind the wheel and for how long. *Cuvva*, the firm that launched the first pay-as-you-go service, estimates the model can save infrequent drivers up to 70 per cent of the cost of an average annual premium, which they claim could be between £500 and £1,500.[2] While established insurance giants have been slow to embrace the idea, it is widely expected this way of paying for our driving could be the norm within the next five years. Other similar services are now appearing, such as *By Miles*.

Ideas like *Cuvva* and *By Miles* (and there are many more where that came from as we will see in this book) are all possible today thanks to the Internet of Things. The Internet of Things is often described in a somewhat flippant way by using the example of a smart fridge that can tell you when you've run out of milk or cheese. However, it is so much more than that. In finance, the Internet of Things represents an amazing opportunity to use the extensive information gathered about us every second to create a potentially endless range of more personal, unique experiences.

Smart thinking, smart banking and the Internet of Things

Let's stick with the smart fridge for the moment but extend the philosophy to see how smart our homes are becoming when it comes to paying for things. Forget about evenings spent home shopping on your laptop at the kitchen table, laboriously filling in your personal details, verifying your credit card details and pressing 'pay now'. That's so, well, yesterday (and things do move fast in fintech, believe me). Buying goods and paying bills via voice-first devices such as Amazon Echo will increasingly become the norm. My own bank has been experimenting with Google Home, integrating our API with the smart speaker so our customers can query their balances and payments via voice commands. Thanks to the Internet of Things and readily available data, everything is just easier to do.

The way we pay for household utilities is changing too. The estimated £1.5 billion in excess funds held by utility giants related to overpaid prepayments will be consigned to the history books thanks to the increased use of smart meters connected to our bank accounts. If funds are tight, it will be possible to set, say, a heating fuel budget. An algorithm could automatically increase or reduce a household's thermostat according to the outside temperature, but also to ensure that the previously set budget is not exceeded. With a connection to your bank account, the thermostat might act with sensitivity to unexpected expenditure or unusual demands on your bank balance rather than any fixed budget you set. It's one less thing for you to worry about managing when tough times come upon you unexpectedly. Again, you will only spend the money you need or are able to spend. Nothing more, nothing less.

When it comes to day-to-day payments, the process of reaching into your purse for credit or debit cards will soon become completely redundant. Just as most people very rarely use cash these days, our reliance on plastic is also on the wane. Consumers are already accustomed to making payments with their phone, or via smart watches such as Apple Watch, or FitBit, but this trend will undoubtedly expand and develop. While most wearables are currently tethered to a smartphone, there is work being done on rings, key fobs and clothing as potential payment devices. There is no doubt that, in future, this will go one stage further and our details and purchases will be secured via an implanted chip, or biometrics such as facial recognition. You won't need to queue to pay either, because these processes will happen automatically as we enter buildings such as museums and cinemas, or as we leave a shop with our goods, with each of our purchases logged and payments being automatically taken from our accounts.

There is no corner of banking and finance that is not being touched in some way by new, data-driven innovations.

There is no corner of banking and finance that is not being touched in some way by these new, data-driven innovations. Even the way we borrow money is changing. Where once we'd be at the mercy of banks who would make lending decisions based on a crude credit score, there are now many more ways to assess the creditworthiness of a borrower, often by analysing activity recorded on their phones. Meanwhile, peer-to-peer lending, where would-be lenders are matched directly to individual or corporate borrowers, has already grown into a £3 billion-plus industry.

Today's fintech innovators are aggressively targeting transactions across the board, using user-friendly interfaces to make processes faster, easier and much cheaper. Mobile money transfer services enable people to bypass bank accounts altogether, transferring cash to each other and merchants via mobile phones.

Individual products for individuals

It is inevitable that our enhanced connectivity will have an impact on every area of our lives, both in and out of the home, making managing our finances a lot, lot easier. Our relationships with financial providers will become far more personalized thanks to the readily available flow of detailed information about each and every one of us. There is less and less need for a one-size-fits-all approach in mortgages, savings policies and pensions. Products will be better geared to who you are and how you spend. Likewise, the marketing of financial products will be much less of a scatter-gun affair. With the volume of information on offer, it is now easier to approach individuals with properly targeted offers, advice and rewards. Gone are the days of a wallet full of plastic 'loyalty cards' (which were only ever a clumsy way to gather customer data, rather than actually rewarding loyalty). We are entering a new era where shops and services are now genuinely presenting rewards and incentives to truly loyal customers that will have a positive and noticeable impact on their wallets.

Shops and services are presenting rewards and incentives to truly loyal customers that will have a positive and noticeable impact on their wallets.

Thanks to beacon technology, which identifies individuals and tracks their behaviour, businesses can push bespoke messages, promotions or personalized offers towards their customers at any time. That's good for businesses and consumers, not just businesses.

One thing is certain: technology is already completely redefining how we use money and run our financial lives, and I only expect this pace of change to accelerate. The next raft of financial solutions will most likely extend far beyond day-to-day financial services as we have traditionally known them into entirely new and innovative areas.

Get smarter: with your pocket bank manager

If you are not already taking advantage of the advances that we've just looked at, there is nothing to prevent you getting started right now. If you own a smartphone, you are already the potential beneficiary of a whole raft of bespoke personal finance advice options that are available to you at any time and in any location. In fact, you could look upon your smartphone as your very own, permanent financial adviser. It is rather like having a (very well-informed) personal bank manager in your pocket. These handheld gadgets are a brilliant source of free advice 24/7, which will steer you towards ever more effective money management. If you take advantage of just some of the fintech products that actively assist you to look at your expenditure and what is on offer at any one time, you will automatically be better off.

Your pocket bank manager's role shouldn't be restricted to saving and managing money more efficiently either. As well as doing the basics, such as checking balances, alerting you to better deals and advising on how to pay off debts, it only requires just a few key taps to uncover neat, money saving tips. You could set it up to signal when it is time to switch utility provider, or change credit card to save x amount of interest. It can also actively work with you to make sure you don't get into financial trouble. By combining knowledge of your daily and monthly spend with predictions of your future behaviour, your pocket bank manager could issue a polite reminder that if you carry on spending at a particular rate, you will not be able to meet, say, your rent bill obligation next month. Evolving AI products will increasingly come into their own when it comes to continually looking out for your well-being, so you can rest easy in the knowledge that you have enough in your pension pot or to pay for big financial goals.

The possibilities of this disruption really are endless, and interesting new apps are coming out day by day that tackle every possible area of finances and beyond. The sky really is the limit. At Starling Bank we have hackathon events, where we work with outside developers to help them make use of the capabilities we open up to them. One neat potential future application that cropped up at one of these was a clever idea by MABLE Forge that was designed for families to help elderly relatives who might be in the early stages of dementia. The app would track the spending patterns of the dementia sufferer (with their permission) and, if unusual patterns emerged, relatives could be alerted that there may be a looming issue. This is, as I say, just one of hundreds of new ideas coming out all the time. In this book, we'll be looking at many similar, innovative ideas that have made it all the way to launch, but it is well worth keeping an eye out to see what else is happening in areas that specifically affect you and your family. Finding the right app could make the world of difference to your future cash position and circumstances.

Without a doubt, banking has come a long way from the days when we had to queue up in branches just to draw out our spending money. Thanks to the relentless innovation of disruptors, we are experiencing a revolution in the way we save, spend and manage our cash. It's a big challenge for an industry that has historically changed very slowly, but there are a growing number of new fintechs vying to completely change everything about money.

Notes

1   Accenture [accessed 11 January 2017] Financial providers: Transforming distribution models for the evolving consumer [Online] www.accenture.com/t20170111T041601__w__/us-en/_acnmedia/ Accenture/next-gen-3/DandM-Global-Research-Study/Accenture-Financial-Services-Global-Distribution-Marketing-Consumer-Study.pdf

2   Cuvva website: www.cuvva.com

CHAPTER THREE

Love your data

It's the key to your financial health

Data is empowering

Data is scary, right? Well, it certainly appears to be so in banking terms anyhow. While most of us are perfectly happy to share an inordinate amount of our personal details on apps and websites such as Facebook, LinkedIn, SnapChat or Twitter, the brakes usually go on as soon as anything money orientated comes along.

Don't feel guilty. Banks have been banging the drum for years about not sharing your details. Doing so will simply leave you wide open to fraud, right? Give away your personal details and it is akin to leaving the front door wide open when you go out for the day.

Yet, while there are some good reasons to be cautious, are we being over-cautious? And, more importantly, are financial institutions encouraging some somewhat muddled thinking here? I believe they are and it is to all of our detriments. Not *all* information sharing is bad. We shouldn't close our minds to the exceptional opportunities afforded by sharing data. Data is empowering.

First though, a short (financial) health warning: this is not an encouragement to throw caution to the wind and forget basic security concerns! Everyone has a part to play when it comes to preventing fraud. This is not a section encouraging you to give your banking password or credit card pin number to all and sundry. Or, indeed, *anyone*. No, what I am talking about here is your transaction data, in other words what you do with your money and indeed time on a day-to-day basis. Your life and the way you spend it and your money creates a vast volume of data, which is known as big data. The data I'm referring to here refers to the extremely large sets of digital data that can be analysed to reveal patterns, trends and associations about our behaviour and interactions.

Once upon a time, the most that businesses could hope to know about you was the equivalent to the information you'd use today to apply for a mortgage: essentially your credit score, household size and household income. Today, your online profile goes well beyond those mortgage application basics. By 2020, 1.7 megabytes a second of new information will be created for every human being on the planet.[1]

The quantity of data being produced by each and every one of us is now so large it can't be mined, organized or analysed by human skills alone. The sheer volume means complex digital gathering and analysis tools are required. However, now the machines are involved, businesses know more about you than you'd ever think possible. Thanks to a plethora of internet sources, where you are happy to freely share your information, such as social media, online shopping sites and business forums, it is possible to assess and categorize you with swathes of information you willingly put out there yourself. Every time you post

Businesses know more about you than you'd ever think possible.

your story on Twitter, Snapchat or Facebook, whether it is an announcement of an engagement, pictures of your first home, or your new baby, the information steadily continues to build a picture. You'll be amazed at how much many organizations know about you. Data is also gathered from magazines that sell subscriber data, via online surveys you take of your own free will and through apps on your smartphone. While developers often post their apps for free, the price of entry is the personal information you give out when you use them.

If you are feeling a bit uncomfortable reading this: don't be. This is, believe it or not, something to be celebrated, certainly in terms of the new financial freedoms we've been discussing here. The reason we should be happy about this is because data presents an almost infinite range of opportunities for the financial industry and, in turn, you the consumer. After all, the more information businesses know about you, the better they can tailor their products to your individual needs. They can develop the best range of products and services that will help you make the most of your money.

Data presents an almost infinite range of opportunities for the financial industry and you the consumer.

Besides, making the most out of our data is nothing new. The practice was pioneered by Dunnhumby, a company set up by husband and wife partnership Clive Humby and Edwina Dunn. One of Dunnhumby's first key clients was the supermarket chain Tesco, which launched its Clubcard loyalty card in 1994 in a bid to overtake the UK's then number one grocer Sainsbury's. After Dunnhumby ran a successful trial analysing shoppers' buying habits through their Clubcard records, Tesco's then chairman Lord MacLaurin was quoted as saying that Dunnhumby had learned more about his customers in three months than he had after 30 years at the retailer.

While the concept of making the most out of big data has been gaining momentum ever since, some sections of the finance sector (in particular banks) have been slow to embrace its potential. I suspect the reason why banks have perpetuated the catch-all fear that sharing anything, ANYTHING, about your financial situation is wrong and potentially hazardous, is because they see it as another threat to their business model. Why? Well, once more is known and understood about your day-to-day spending habits, there is an opportunity for a rival firm to pop up and say: 'Hey, I understand what your goals are, and, after looking at your situation, have a better deal for you.'

Fortunately, this pressure to keep absolutely everything to ourselves is becoming increasingly outdated. Data is at the heart of the money revolution and sharing it is what drives the fintech industry and allows all these innovative new products to be launched and constantly refined and improved. While this is great for the companies launching all these services, it is also great for you, the consumer. Sharing your data is the key to giving you more control over your money than ever before. We all need to think positively about data and embrace it, because it has already brought us some great new innovations and is set to bring us many more.

Perhaps we simply need to be more open about data. Or maybe the whole idea of 'sharing data' needs to be redefined. Sharing passwords: *wrong*. Sharing information to get a better, more personalized deal: *fantastic*. It makes good sense.

Why data rules

The possibilities really are endless when it comes to big data. We've still only seen a fraction of what can be done because it is still fairly early days in the evolution of fintech. To get some idea of how exciting data sharing could eventually be for consumers of financial products and services, it's worth pausing to look at the impact big data has had on another business in another sector entirely. Amazon has long been a recognized master with big data. The online retail giant has been growing its customer base at a tremendous rate for a decade or more, and a great deal of this is down to its imaginative uses of big data. As a major retailer it has readymade access to a massive amount of data on its customers: names, addresses, payments and search histories. Very early on, the people at Amazon figured out they could expand the business a lot quicker (and therefore make more money) by using statistics garnered from their *entire* customer database to work out what you as an individual were going to do next. In a nutshell, this is what big data is all about.

Amazon has honed their techniques over the years and they are now absolute experts. It's not a case of them simply pinpointing that a customer is a 30-year-old woman from Swansea, and so is highly likely to have similar buying habits as other 30-year-old females from Swansea. That approach is far too much of a blunt instrument today. No, the retailer looks at everything a customer buys, the day of the month they buy the goods and the time of day: all in real time. Rather than analysing data in hindsight, the new way of doing things is to analyse actions as they happen to predict future actions. With so much information available, the forecasts are extremely accurate.

After gathering a rich vein of data, Amazon customers are matched to other similar consumers in the database. Those customers may be 20, 40 or 60 years old, male or female, but the important thing is they have similar buying habits. Amazon will then target a large group of, say, 10,000 consumers with specific offers. That's why those 'you might like this' offers that pop up on your PC are always so unerringly accurate. Their algorithms have come to the conclusion that as a keen cook, with a new house, you are extremely likely to buy something for your kitchen at the beginning of the month. And it is highly likely that you probably will click on the link they show you. Human beings are very suggestible, especially if the offer is this well tailored.

Fintech firms are working towards doing very much the same sort of thing. Now financial institutions are learning more about their customers' habits and needs, they can cater to them in a more meaningful way. Whereas banks were once simply trying to sell banking, financial and insurance products to customers, regardless of whether they needed those particular products or not, they now have the advantage of understanding each and every customer thoroughly. They carefully study insights into their spending habits before offering them personalized products and services that meet their true needs. They are embracing our data to predict the behaviour of existing customers and pairing them up with other, like-minded individuals on their databases to carefully target them with the most appropriate products and services, whether it is the financial institution's own product or that of a selected partner. Analysis can even be used to determine the exact time of day or night when it is most compelling to present offers to consumers that are tailored to their specific circumstances. Say, for example, you are looking for a loan. In the past, lenders have relied on credit scores to predict consumer behaviour and their ability to pay back the loan. However, now they are armed with a more complete customer profile and a greater understanding of how people like you usually behave, banks and loan companies can match offers in line with the risk of taking on an individual account.

Analysis can even be used to determine the exact time of day or night to present tailored offers to consumers.

Likewise, if financial services providers know you are one of a group of consumers who are not in the least bit concerned about planning for retirement yet, it won't waste money inundating you with messages about pensions or long-term investment products. It is a win-win for both sides, because these firms don't waste their marketing resources, and consumers don't get swamped with unnecessary junk in their inboxes.

Recommendation systems have a key role to play here. With the sheer quantity of products and services growing all the time, it can all get a little overwhelming for those on the receiving end of marketing efforts. It can frequently feel like there is too much information to handle, which leaves many people not doing anything at all about what could be a crucial financial decision. In this scenario, who wouldn't welcome a personalized and apparently thoughtful recommendation based on their spending and saving history?

Arguably, banks are better placed than any other organization, in any other sector, when it comes to big data. After all, they have far, far more information about their customers than even firms like Amazon. They possess a wealth of detail on how much we all spend on a weekly, monthly and yearly basis, and on how we manage our finances. In fact, they are in a unique position because they know exactly what sort of thing you like to spend your cash on. Analyse this data thoroughly and it is possible to offer a completely customized service.

Banks are better placed than any other organization, in any other sector, when it comes to big data.

Say, for example, you opened a savings account with £500. Without the benefit of big data, it is quite possible that a bank will not be all that attentive. They'll probably communicate no more than is necessary and almost certainly won't offer any investment advice. However, if you do actually have many other assets, investments and other savings elsewhere, big data will help the banking systems identify you as a wealthier customer and may be more proactive as a result. With access to the facts, financial firms can see the bigger picture and maximize a customer's potential. Once again, this is to the customer's advantage too.

Using big data, financial products and services can be continuously adjusted and improved. Thanks to social media it is now far easier to monitor how customers feel about what they've bought. That information can be used to adjust products and services to increase positive feedback and customer satisfaction.

Data analysis tools are now able to make use of the huge amounts of meaningful communication data from social media networks. Think your financial services partner is not listening to what you really want from them? They are now. Similarly, expect the providers of financial services to be watching out for how engaged you are with their products. Big data provides valuable clues to the fact you, the consumer, might be about to move on or change accounts. This is known as 'churn' in marketing. If a customer shows specific behaviour connected with cancelling an account, they shouldn't be surprised if their bank is suddenly very attentive indeed.

Where data really comes into its own in financial services is in the development of new products. One of the most interesting steps forward for the disruptors that now shape this industry is something called 'open banking'. In Europe, open banking has been encouraged by an EU Directive with the less-than-inspiring title of Payment Service Directive Two (PSD2). If its name is uninspiring, it's impact should certainly not be. It aims to level the playing field for payment service providers such as banks and financial services companies, to make payments safer and more secure, and to protect consumers. Most interestingly, it provides for customers to give permission to selected companies to access certain parts of their banking data, which in turn opens up access to payment services and transaction data to third parties. This promotes better competition across the board, which will significantly drive innovation.

Don't worry if you've never heard of open banking or don't really understand the ins and outs of how it works. You'll be in good company. An Equifax study[2] found that 90 per cent of consumers had not heard of it. The important thing is (and the reason why we should all be excited about it), if all goes to plan, it should free up a whole host of data, so forward-thinking new fintechs can keep coming up with exciting new products to make all of our financial lives better. The increased competition brought about by sharing data should bring about a wholesale improvement in banking services.

If financial institutions are willing to provide application programming interfaces (APIs), talented developers are able to get in there and build new and innovative applications on the back of the data. This has nothing to do with committing fraud and everything to do with making financial apps better, according to how consumers actually use them. The open banking movement is to everyone's advantage because it paves the way for the creation of a new generation of (ever improved) apps, without each developer having to start from scratch each time to reinvent the wheel. It's great for banks and financial institutions because they'll be able to develop new revenue streams, and it's great for customers because they'll get easier-to-use new services and products that answer their actual needs.

The open banking movement is paving the way for the creation of a new generation of (ever improved) apps.

Take as an example the improvements that have been made to the humble current account. Today, it is not uncommon for people to have more than one current account. You might have your 'main' day-to-day account, which is where your salary gets paid and you manage your monthly outgoings like mortgage or rent, subscriptions, gym membership and cash spending. If you are in a relationship, there might be a joint account where you pool resources to share monthly bills. Then, there may be a separate account for savings, or one for things you like to keep separate like business expenses and so on. Thanks to data sharing, mobile banking services now enable consumers to see everything they have, in each individual account, in one place, even if those accounts are held with different banks. You'll have a complete snapshot of all your monthly spend, on one single screen, without needing to trawl through a number of different sources. Simple things like this make your life and money management a lot, lot easier.

There are a lot of other ways sharing data makes our lives more convenient too. Say, for example, a mobile bank has a selection of mortgage brokers in its marketplace. Thanks to PSD2, customers can opt to share their data with the mortgage brokers their bank works with in order to simplify the whole process. The mortgage broker will have real-time access to the bank customer's financial situation, and will therefore be able to quickly recommend the best possible deal without the customer having to go through a mound of paperwork and checks beforehand. Plus, since the bank will have already KYC'd the customer (the industry term for Know Your Customer, which is the process of identifying and verifying the identity of clients), it can pass this assurance onto the mortgage broker, thus greatly simplifying and shortening the timescale of the whole process. In other words, customers won't need to undergo the exact same checks time after time.

Your app store bank

To me, one of the most exciting parts of data sharing in the new disruptive model in finance is the opportunity to be at the centre of customers' financial lives. With a veritable smorgasbord of new financial products on the block, and many more being introduced all the time, there needs to be a 'marketplace' where customers can view everything on offer and find out what suits their particular situation best. My vision has been that banks will be at the centre of it all, working rather like an 'app store' to enable customers to easily view and select other financial services from insurance to mortgages provided by carefully selected third parties.

To visualize how this works, I always imagine a good quality market such as you might find in any town or city centre near you. This is a place where individuals and small businesses come to sell foodstuffs, from excellent coffee to fine cheeses. For the customer, it is a great commercial hub in which to stroll around and select the best produce. Naturally, people will choose the stuff that appeals to them most, or which is appropriate to, say, the meal they are planning that evening. As they make their purchases, they will have a relationship with the individual stalls they buy from, but it is the market that has brought them all together. In the future, it is very likely that banks will take the market role, bringing together financial brands and services that they are proud to work with and who are likewise proud to be associated with them.

Starling Bank, for example, already has more than two dozen (and counting) partnerships with third-party financial services providers, from insurers, to wealth managers, to savings and investment providers. We have our core current account product and offer our customers a wide range of services on top of that through our hub. I predict we will see many more models like this emerging over the next few years as banks understand their new role at the core of a customer's relationship with money.

It is likely that banks will take the 'market role', bringing together financial brands and services they are proud to work with and who are likewise proud to be associated with them.

The marketplace model I have described here may not be confined solely to financial services either. In our more connected world, it is quite probable your banking app could develop to become the centre of a much wider range of products or services. Take a motoring app for example. Wouldn't it be useful to seamlessly integrate it with all the financial transactions around your car, so you could see at a glance how much is being spent on motor insurance, petrol and indeed all your running costs. It is so much easier to stay on top of expenditure when you live in a more connected world.

If you are feeling uncomfortable about sharing your data far and wide, don't be. Banks need to secure your go-ahead before sharing any details with each separate provider. There is no carte blanche permission to distribute your details far and wide. Data may have been used unscrupulously in certain instances in the past, but the innovation behind open banking is there to put you, the customer, back in control of your own data. If you are not happy to share, don't. Like I say though, the positives generally greatly outweigh the negatives.

It is also worth mentioning that, perhaps ironically given concerns over sharing and potential criminal activity, big data also means our accounts are substantially less susceptible to fraud. Better use of data means our account transactions can be viewed in real time. Banks already use analytics to differentiate between legitimate transactions and unusual or potentially unauthorized ones, which will be spotted immediately. The analysis system takes immediate action, blocking irregular transactions, stopping fraud before it happens.

The central premise of the new rules around data is that we should all enjoy better deals from financial institutions, more secure payments, and easier and more transparent management of our day-to-day financial affairs. Plus, if financial firms open up customers' account data to third-party providers (with customers' authorization, of course) it will mean that the rate of development and disruption will continue at its present exciting trajectory.

This is all just the beginning. There are many, many more imaginative uses of big data coming through in the finance industry, and it will have a significant impact on banks and financial services. Once again, it is being driven by you, the consumer. Consumers, not companies, are driving business decisions (at long last).

Notes

1 McKinsey (2017) *Analytics in Banking: Time to realize the value*, McKinsey, New York
2 Equifax [accessed 24 January 2017] Use of personal data [Online] www.equifax.com

PART TWO

Fintech money makeover

CHAPTER FOUR

Check your credit score

There are not many people who are not aware of credit scores or how important it is to keep them in good shape. So far, so good. Unfortunately, where it all begins to unravel is when there is a lot of misunderstanding about what 'good shape' actually means. Somewhere along the line the view seems to have developed that a credit score is a measure of financial stability. In other words, a high credit score is a badge of wealth, while a low one is associated with those who are poor. This is, in fact, a complete misinterpretation.

A credit score is simply the metric by which the banking industry determines how well people handle debt and therefore whether they are a worthy candidate for a loan or mortgage. The score, which is just three figures long, tells financial providers if a particular person is a good bet so they can make money out of doing business with them.

Having a good credit score doesn't automatically mean you are wealthy. Amazon founder Jeff Bezos could apply for bankruptcy tomorrow (unlikely I know, but bear with me) and this would decimate his credit score. However, this wouldn't mean he was broke. He'd still have many billions in assets. The (shock!) bankruptcy would simply indicate that he was unlikely to pay his bills.

Likewise, Joe Bloggs may have a fantastic credit score because he always appears to pay his bills promptly. Look more closely though and his finances could be in a mess. He may actually have a negative net worth because of all the money he owes to a long list of creditors. Or, Michelle Moneybags may be a millionaire, but she might also have a shockingly low credit rating. Why? Because she never uses credit. She pays off any credit cards in full each month, doesn't have a mortgage and has no need of loans. She has never demonstrated her ability to stay on top of debts.

So, forget the misconceptions. When it all comes down to it, your creditworthiness comes down to how you handle debt. It is not a badge of honour (or otherwise) that says anything about your net worth.

Wealth indication is not the only myth about credit scoring, which doesn't really help the general misunderstanding about the process. There is, for example, no such thing as a *universal* credit score and, more importantly, there are no credit score blacklists for people who are banned from any sort of borrowing for the rest of their lives for some sort of financial misdemeanour. Each lender has a different (and largely top secret) way of scoring would-be borrowers. A range of tools is used to work out whether or not to lend to each individual. This includes inspecting credit files sourced from credit reference agencies (of which more see below), the information supplied with a loan application and even any records of past dealings the lender may have had with an applicant. If one lender rejects an application, it doesn't mean that all the others will automatically do the same. It doesn't work that way.

For clarification, if anyone has had a history of defaulting or late payments, it may *feel* like they are on a credit blacklist, because many organizations will be wary of lending money in these circumstances. However, there are many firms that will lend in this situation, albeit at a higher interest rate than elsewhere.

The confusion over what credit scoring is all about isn't helped by the fact that most lenders do very little to help us understand what's what. And to make matters worse, credit reference agencies depend on a certain amount of nervousness about ratings, so they can sell consumers extra services to keep an eye on their scores.

So, for much needed clarity, let me just explain briefly how it works before we go into the digital developments. In the UK, consumers are subject to three different credit scores from three separate credit reference agencies: Experian, Equifax and Callcredit. In the United States it is Experian, Equifax and TransUnion. If you request scores from each one, the result would be different in each case. This is mainly because not all lenders report to, or share details with, the same credit reference agency. In the UK, for example, HSBC passes on information to Experian and Equifax, but not to Callcredit, whereas NatWest and Barclays report to all three. According to MoneySavingExpert.com figures, 55 per cent of lenders use Equifax, 77 per cent use Experian and 34 per cent use Callcredit.

The agencies all have different maximum scores too. Experian's score is out of 999, Equifax's is 700 and Callcredit's is 710. It is difficult to correlate between the three because they have different scoring scales too. So, your credit score may be, say, 459 with Equifax, 997 with Experian and 600 with Callcredit.

Your personal credit score is calculated on a number of factors. First, there is your payment history, so if there is a pattern of regularly not paying bills on time your score will suffer. The way you've used credit in the past is another element that has an impact. Lenders look at your financial history too to check whether or not you have always paid back any loans on time and in full. Something that would automatically raise a red flag among nearly every lender is a slew of recent credit applications. This sort of thing can be perceived as an early indicator of financial problems, and that naturally makes lenders nervous.

But why is this important? you may think. *It is what it is and I can't do a huge amount about it, so why worry?* Let me tackle the first part of the question to begin with. Credit scores are crucial because, sooner or later, most of us do rely on credit in some shape or form. After all, without borrowings, most people wouldn't be able to buy a house or even a car.

Even if you are not making a significant purchase, credit scores can have a huge impact on the life decisions we all make. If, for example, you are trying to rent a house or apartment, landlords invariably use credit reports to screen potential tenants. They need to know that applicants are good for the rent.

In all these cases, a credit score needs to be sufficiently respectable to convince a third party that you are good for the cash. Having a bad credit score can adversely affect you in a number of ways, over and above that of being turned down for a mortgage, loan or a rental. In fact, ironically, it can even contribute to you being financially worse off. Insurance companies, particularly car insurers, use credit scores when determining rates. A poor credit score could see a premium rocket. Likewise, when it comes to credit cards, credit scores don't just dictate whether an applicant is accepted or rejected, but also whether or not they are given promotional rates and a decent APR after that. A poor credit history could mean more pressure is heaped on via a punitive interest rate on future advances. There are even certain jobs that are not open to applicants who have a bad credit history. Financial services, or indeed any sort of role requiring some sort of financial management, are the most obvious in this respect, and many firms do now take credit history into account when they employ people. It should be noted that they do have to ask permission to access your credit report before doing so.

As you can see, your credit score is important in a range of different ways. Which brings me to the second part of the question I posed earlier: why worry when there is nothing you can do about it? There is, in fact, much you can do to improve your situation and maintain a good score. The most obvious by far is to always be on time making payments and never miss one. Missing out on just one or two payments can affect your rating for years. Defaults in the previous 12 months will have the biggest impact. (See Chapter 10 'Bill management made easy' for advice on a range of apps that will help you keep things on track with bills.)

There are ways you can actively boost your credit score too. If you have old credit cards that have a zero balance but are still open, this can help keep your credit history looking good. Lenders like to see that a person relies on a good mix of credit. If someone has a few credit cards, a mortgage, a car loan and so on, it all counts in their favour.

It is also well worth remembering that if you have a joint financial product with a partner, whether it is a mortgage or joint account, their files can be accessed and looked at as part of any assessment into your score. You can even be co-scored on a joint bills account with flatmates, which could leave you in a vulnerable position. It stands to reason that if your partner or flatmate has a poor credit history, you might want to think about keeping your finances completely separate. If you do part ways from someone with whom you've had joint finances and think it prudent to uncouple your financial history too, write to each of the three credit reference agencies and ask for a notice of disassociation.

Most importantly though, keep a regular check on your credit score.

Stay on top of your credit score – for free

Credit reference agencies hold enormous amounts of data on you, and errors can and do creep into the records. It can happen surprisingly easily too. Say, for example, you are filling in an application form and accidently mark your salary as £2,500 instead of £25,000. Who doesn't make this sort of innocent, decimal point error now and again? Unfortunately, that missing zero will play havoc with credit files, particularly if you have noted your salary correctly elsewhere on other forms. Inconsistencies like this, or listing slightly different job titles each time, or spelling names incorrectly, alert automated fraud scoring processes that something is not quite right here.

Unfortunately, these sorts of basic human errors are notoriously hard to unravel. Not only will you probably have no clue what you've done wrong, but firms are awful at explaining the real reason why they have turned someone down.

If you want to keep on top of your credit score, the best advice is to check with all three credit reference agencies. Everyone should do this at least once a year, and it is highly recommended that you do it again if there is a big application in the offing. This way it is possible to note any potential errors and correct them before they become an issue.

Oh, and don't worry that checking on your score will adversely impact your rating: this is another credit score myth. Checking your own credit score is generally counted as a 'soft inquiry', which means there is no 'hard pull' on your credit report. 'Hard pulls' usually happen when you apply for a new credit card or submit an application for a mortgage or general loan. Soft pulls occur in such cases as when a potential employer does a background check on an individual, or when someone is pre-approved for a credit card.

There are a wide range of services on offer that can be used to check your personal credit scores. Some of them cost money, while some don't. It doesn't necessarily follow that you have to pay top dollar in order to get the best, most in-depth report.

So what are the options?

We all have the legal right to access our credit report from a credit reference agency in exchange for a small fee. In the UK the fee is £2. These reports offer a basic snapshot of a person's credit history but won't include a credit score. All three credit reference agencies also offer more comprehensive reports for a monthly fee. This includes unlimited access to your credit report, plus a handful of extra features such as the actual credit score and alerts whenever any major changes to the report occur.

There are also opportunities to access both your credit report and score without having to pay for a subscription. Equifax offers a 30-day trial of its CreditExpert service, which gives full access to credit reports, the score and then any subsequent email alerts about any changes to the file. Once the trial ends though, it costs £14.99 a month to maintain the service. You could, of course, sign up, check your score and then cancel before the fees kick in. Experian offers a similar 30-day trial, which costs £9.95 once the free period ends. Alternatively, it is possible to get the Equifax report for free through Clearscore. The company makes its money via commission on products on its website. Finally, Callcredit reports and scores are available free via its Noddle service, which also maintains the service by advertising loans and cards.

Each of the above have apps, so it is easy to check and monitor your credit score situation.

Best for: independent credit score apps

Separately, there are also a number of free apps that are not directly connected to the credit reference agencies but that do broadly the same thing. *Totally Money* uses data from two of the three credit agencies (Experian and Callcredit). It also shows money that has been borrowed on mortgages, credit cards and overdrafts with up to six years of back records available. What is useful is the app has a live data feed. So, every time you log in, it updates the report for an up-to-date snapshot of the financial position. There are also notifications if something changes too, so if anything is not going as expected, it can be quickly cleared up. Thus, if you miss a monthly payment, for example, it is a useful nudge to get it sorted out as quickly as possible. *Totally Money* also lets you know your 'borrowing power' and what lenders would think of you should you apply.

If you are becoming a bit of a credit score junkie, you may like the US *Credit.com* app, which not only gives a free credit score and report card but also features articles on how it all works, how you can improve your score and which products you can use to borrow. You can even submit questions that might be answered in future articles. The *CreditKarma* app offers the usual services such as free credit score reports and alerts, but has the useful additional service of allowing consumers to file a dispute direct from the app. *CreditWise* is a free credit scoring app connected to the American bank Capital One, but you don't need to buy a Capital One product to download and use it. *CreditWise* has an interesting extra: a credit simulator, which shows how actions such as paying off debt could affect your score. There are also personalized suggestions for improving credit scores.

Apps for that: *Totally Money, Credit.com, CreditKarma, CreditWise*

Digital credit scores

Credit scores are all well and good when the one you have is OK. People in this situation no doubt think that the whole system works swimmingly well. They apply for a loan/mortgage/credit card, credit checks are done and the paperwork is drawn up. Simple, right?

When you have a bad credit score though, it can quickly become a huge impediment. Millions of people around the world have a credit score too low to make them eligible for credit from banks today. There are vast numbers who are considered 'credit invisible', meaning they have no credit history with the main ratings agencies. In the United States, for example, more than 25 million Americans are locked into a situation where the credit score model discounts them from all loans at a stroke.

If you are one of the fortunate ones whose credit rating is OK, you may not think this concerns you. However, it should. In fact, everyone should be alert to the reliance on credit scores in the digital world. The chances are, if things don't move with the times, nearly everyone will end up with a poor rating.

As the present system stands, the big ratings bureaus each rely on very similar metrics. They are interested in what you've paid for, what you own and how promptly you pay off your bills. Yet, in a world where the payment structure is changing by the minute, this is looking increasingly outdated. How do the existing metrics cope with peer-to-peer exchange, global transfer, or mobile phone transactions? These are all payment methods that are being increasingly relied upon. Many millennials may not have the credit history needed to make big purchases if their parents and guardians have helped them with expenses for most of their lives, which is often the case. This means there will be little credit information for lenders to fall back on.

While credit histories are without a doubt useful, the definition of 'good credit' is changing and widening, and there are no signs the credit ratings agencies are keeping pace at the moment. Yet, as time goes on and we further embrace new ways of paying for things, it will become increasingly apparent that there need to be other ways to judge a loan candidate than just a credit history.

Fortunately, we are already witnessing the beginnings of more innovative ways of looking at credit. The handful of independent apps featured in the previous section demonstrate the beginnings of a far broader approach to the previously black and white, good or bad, credit score. The trend is moving towards helping consumers help themselves, with apps providing tools to allow users to do things such as assisting in challenging wrong or unfair decisions, or showing how different actions can help their case.

Even so, the changes don't go far enough. The focus in the immediate future is to find a way to deliver credit to people who would normally be discounted and then move towards working out how to assess people in the digital economy. What is required is an entirely new way of assessing individuals. Once again, data is a huge help. Fintechs are turning their gaze to a wide range of other useful indicators that can be found within the multiple streams of information now available about all of us. Details such as where we shop and our spending histories, as well as who is in our network of friends, all work together to build a far more comprehensive and truthful picture of our creditworthiness. Gathering data across various bank accounts gives a far greater insight into transaction histories. As the use of machine learning increases, data and advances in analytics will inevitably see fintechs gain ground where credit checks are concerned.

To date, the earliest innovations in this respect have focused primarily on the business loans market. Many start-ups in this area are already ignoring individual credit scores altogether when determining whether to lend or not. They examine behaviour and data and compare it to the applicant's peer group for a greater understanding of what might actually happen. Companies such as *PayPal*, *Kabbage*, *SmartBiz* and *Square* all offer new ways of looking at creditworthiness. More details on these lenders can be found in Chapter 14 'Borrow clever' about loans.

Best for: applicants with no or poor credit history

But, what if you are an individual with a less than glowing credit report? Well, once again, there are signs of a growing interest in what can be done to help people like this. *Petal* is a new credit card built by a New York-based fintech and it has no fees and high credit limits. *Petal* relies on machine learning and uses a newly created algorithm to analyse a borrower's digital financial record. While it still takes into account credit records, it also looks at how much an applicant earns, saves and spends, and the bills they pay each month. It aims for full transparency, so if a card holder decides not to pay off a balance, it shows the exact dollar amount of the interest they'll be liable to pay. *Petal* charges an interest rate of 15.24 per cent to 26.24 per cent APR on purchases, which compares favourably with other credit cards for those without a credit score, which charge APRs of up to 29.99 per cent.

App for that: *Petal*

Best for: 'credit invisible'

The greatest focus of innovation in this area has been in regions whose populations have an unusually high proportion of people who have never appeared on public credit agencies: the so-called 'credit invisible'. This is where a person may very well be a good credit risk, yet he or she struggles to find a way to prove it to a lender. This is something that has particularly affected those in developing markets where access to finance is more limited, but it has also blighted those in more buoyant economies.

Mobile phones have been identified as having an outstanding potential to play a role in gathering enough useful information to develop alternative credit scores. Not only do close to 100 per cent of people in most areas have one but phones also contain a wealth of information that goes well beyond their original function of making calls and sending messages. People use their mobiles for contact lists, calendars, internet surfing, social media and plenty more besides. All of these activities provide crucial data for behavioural analytics.

In India, for example, where 250 million adults out of a population of 1.3 billion people have no access to a bank account and even more have no credit scores at all, *Cashe* offers personal loans to young people who have just entered the workforce. Applicants answer a set of questions to apply, and data from their mobile phone records counts towards assessing the application. *ZestMoney* focuses on micro loans for single purchase items and uses a combination of mobile tech, digital banking and AI to vet the 200,000 plus applications per month. In China, internet retail giant Alibaba has launched *Hua Bei*, or 'just spend', which is a mini loan provider. In a country where only 25 per cent of the population have a credit history, the remaining 75 per cent are being viewed as a potentially lucrative battleground if big data can provide a reliable alternative to the traditional credit scoring model. East Africans now have access to *Tala*, which collects data about phone owners and uses the data points to make lending decisions. With phone ownership rising steadily, this creates a huge opportunity for the 90 per cent of people who do not have a credit score.

These under-served regions are leading the way when it comes to rethinking the increasingly outdated reliance on credit scores.

Apps for that: *Cashe, ZestMoney, Hua Bei, Tala*

CHAPTER FIVE

Make money every time you shop

Loyalty

In recent years, a general 'loyalty malaise' has inevitably grown among the shopping public. You know the sort of thing: this is where you end up with so much plastic in your purse/wallet, you can barely stand to hunt out the right card when you are asked for it at the checkout. In fact, nearly a fifth of consumers won't have redeemed their points in the past 12 months.[1] In the UK, it is estimated that of the three most popular schemes, Tesco Clubcard, Nectar and Boots Advantage, there are £4.5 billion worth of loyalty points lying dormant.

Part of the apathy is down to the fact the novelty factor has definitely worn off. After all, loyalty programmes are nothing new. In their first incarnation as trading stamps in the 1950s they were intended to be used as a marketing tool to give customers an extra incentive to come back and spend more money with a particular store. Green Shield Stamps were the first of such schemes, and many people of the generation that collected them will recount stories of painstakingly sticking down the small paper stamps into dog-eared books in order to exchange them for gifts chosen from a catalogue. It wasn't until the 1990s that businesses began to cotton on to the other enormous value of these schemes: namely, that they offer a vast amount of information about individual customers and their spending habits. In the UK it was grocery giant Tesco that pioneered the plastic loyalty card scheme called Clubcard where, instead of gifts, loyalty was rewarded with a small amount of money off subsequent purchases at Tesco. As I described in Chapter 3, the supermarket giant worked with Dunnhumby to mine acres of data detailing the minutiae of our individual shopping habits that was all gleaned from Clubcard. Not surprisingly, this tactic was promptly copied by every other high street rival. These loyalty cards, in turn, spawned a range of online schemes, where customers could sign up and gain points. Again, this proliferated across the spectrum, so you could gain points for doing anything from filling up your car, to visiting a spa, to buying a cappuccino. And all the while, the stock of data on our shopping movements and preferences piled up.

The more innovative among the retailers on the high street know that the pressure is on to keep shoppers in tune with the idea of loyalty. The solution that some outlets have come up with is to integrate loyalty into a wider 'lifestyle' app. Starbucks' app is a great example of this. As well as being the platform for its rewards programme, customers can also use the coffee shop's app to place and pay for orders, and even access streamed music. Members of the programme earn stars towards rewards, which can be redeemed in real time. The whole package is geared towards reinforcing Starbucks' 'lifestyle enhancement' brand.

Undoubtedly, one of the most successful among the new breed of loyalty programmes is Amazon Prime. Initially, the annual membership fee for the programme simply guaranteed free shipping, but now it offers a huge range of benefits from live streaming music, movies and TV shows, to storage for digital photos.

By paying for membership, customers are invariably steered towards buying more from the retailer.

All the signs are that there is more to come. Loyalty is entering another creative stage, and it might pay for you to take a look at what's on offer these days.

Best for: keeping track of loyalty points

If you are the sort of person who has loyally (ahem) hung onto all your plastic cards, there are now ways to keep track of them without keeping them all in a bulging wallet. Apps such as *Perkd*, *Snappcard* or *Stocard* allow you to keep all your loyalty cards in a single app. Simply scan your loyalty cards and they will be added into a digital wallet. Then, when you shop, present your phone to the person at the till when they ask for your loyalty card and let them scan it. The apps can store hundreds of cards, so there is no excuse to miss out on perks wherever you shop, even if you only visit a particular store on a very occasional basis. It's certainly a neater and more efficient way of keeping track of what you have, so you know what your points are worth and when you can spend them.

Apps for that: *Perkd, Snappcard, Stocard*

Best for: integrating points into banking apps

It's possible to make your life easier still with a new generation of apps that make collecting and redeeming loyalty points still more convenient. Indeed, the onus is no longer on you or me to actively redeem points: it is automatically done for you. You barely even need to think about it.

Apps such as *Flux*, *Tail* and *Yoyo Wallet* integrate loyalty points into supporting banking apps. All you need to do is buy your goods at stores that support the apps (check for an up-to-date list, but currently retail partners that work with these apps include Café Nero, Eat, Itsu, Planet Organic, Visa and Costa), and any loyalty rewards due from each purchase will be automatically displayed in your banking app, alongside a fully itemized receipt. You even don't have to pay via your *Flux*, *Tail* or *Yoyo Wallet* app or scan any barcodes; you simply pay with your usual card or phone. Then, when you have accrued enough loyalty to qualify for a reward, your app will send cashback directly into your bank account on behalf of the retailer in question. You really don't need to do a thing. What's great about this development is it overcomes some of the biggest hurdles to a successful two-way loyalty relationship between retailers and their customers: namely, that it is very easy to lose/forget cards, or even forget you've signed up in the first place.

There are plenty of possibilities for loyalty schemes to evolve and improve still further too. Already under discussion are apps that link with the location services in your mobile. Shops could then team up with each other to offer some truly imaginative incentives. Thus, when a consumer buys an energy drink at a health club vending machine, it could prompt a digital coupon for 10 per cent off a pair of running shoes at a nearby sports store. With a bit of imagination, commercial enterprises could transform our somewhat jaded attitude to loyalty and make it a great marketing tool that works as well for you and me as for the businesses themselves.

Apps for that: *Flux*, *Tail*, *Yoyo Wallet*

Cashback

Money off coupons and loyalty points are all very well, but not much beats the joyous experience of being paid cold hard cash as a reward for spending your money on stuff you were already intending to buy. Online and app-based cashback services have been around for a while now, fuelling a US $80 billion global industry,[2] and it is easy to see why. If you are not familiar with how they work, it is all quite simple. First, you need to sign up to a cashback site such as *Topcashback* or *Quidco*. Then, when you want to buy something online, rather than going direct to the retailer's website, go to your chosen cashback website and search for the retailer there. If it is listed – and most major outlets are signed up, from supermarkets to fashion outlets to DIY stores – click the link to visit the company. It's not just traditional retailers either: cashback deals are also on offer that cover all sorts of household bills, such as changing your energy or broadband supplier. Again, simply access the utility via the cashback site and then continue as normal.

Once you enter a site via a cashback operator, your visit to your chosen outlet is then tracked and, if you buy anything, you will receive cashback once the transaction is processed. The sum you get in return is based on a percentage of the sale, with different retailers offering different incentives, but the amount can be significant. After that, it can take a few weeks, or even months, for the sum to arrive in your cashback kitty, but once you get into the habit it can quickly build into a regular tidy sum. Indeed, some people claim to make hundreds of pounds a year out of shopping via cashback sites.

To anyone that has yet to try this money-saving scheme (or even those that have and haven't really thought very much about it), the obvious question is: why do retailers give away money? After all, there is no such thing as something for nothing, right? The short answer is, it is just another in a long list of promotional tools in a store's armoury. The technology behind cashback is fairly simple and therefore low cost to run, and it is a great way for a business to generate leads. It's much cheaper to reward consumers direct with a modest amount of money, rather than spending hundreds of thousands on an advertising campaign that a potential customer may not even see. Rewarding loyalty like this builds a relationship with individual customers and makes it more likely that they will return. The cashback sites are a great way to drive traffic (ie you and me) right to the retailer's website.

Best for: buying online and on the high street

Just like loyalty schemes, the cashback business needs to keep on its toes in order to stay relevant to customers. While the promotion originally began online, it has now been extended to also offer shoppers cashback when they physically visit a high street store. *Topcashback* and *Quidco*, for example, both have schemes where you can earn cashback when you use your credit or debit card instore. With *Quidco High Street* and *Topcashback OnCard* you simply register your usual credit or debit card to your account. When you get to the shop, pay for your goods using your registered card and the retailer will pay commission for your purchase. There is also the facility to browse their websites ahead of your shopping trip in order to activate exclusive offers in the shops you want to visit. Cashback will be paid directly into your account once the purchases are confirmed.

Apps for that: *Topcashback*, *Quidco*

Best for: additional discount offers

One of the newest fintechs into the cashback space is called *Tail*, which works with *Starling* and *Monzo* banks. At the time of writing, the app offers big discounts at places to eat and drink in London and within the M25 area, which are all linked to the card you use to pay the bill. It is quite likely that the geographical reach will extend, as will the breadth of outlets, and I fully expect to see many more cashback apps head in this direction.

To get started with *Tail* you need to grant it access to your digital bank account via a simple one-tap process (if you don't have a *Starling* or *Monzo* account, you can sign up for one for free). Once you've agreed to the T&Cs, browse the app for offers that interest you. The offer feed is updated in real time and is location specific, directing you towards any deals nearby. Any offers that pop up in the *Tail* app are redeemed by simply using your usual bank card at the corresponding merchant. There is no need for coupons, or redirection, or receipt scanning, or even to explicitly 'tell' *Tail* the name of the bank account or card number where you want your cashback deposited. The accumulated savings are simply deposited back into your account at regular intervals.

App for that: *Tail*

Digitized receipts

Wheel your trolley through the automatic double doors of grocery stores such as Aldi or Lidl and you will expect no frills, but great prices. Opt to spend your cash at top-end outlets such as Saks or Selfridges, and you'd rightly expect to pay a bit more, but you can count on attentive service from the moment you engage with shop staff. Visit toy shops such as Lego Store, or Hamleys, or FAO Schwarz, and you'd be forgiven for anticipating a fun-filled dollop of so-called retail theatre. A bit of magic to go with your purchases.

The one constant that remains the same, and which has done so for centuries, is that once you have made your purchase, the cashier will give you a receipt describing who, what, when, where and how whatever you purchased was paid for. The more diligent among you will carefully fold the piece of paper containing this information and pop it into a purse or wallet, perhaps to check later, or to record the sale on a budget plan. More likely though, it'll be tossed into the same bag as the purchase and forgotten about.

Either way, it is pretty certain that you haven't stopped to think: isn't it absurd that we have 21st-century solutions for nearly all aspects of our shopping, from contactless payment to self-service tills, yet we still routinely receive paper receipts in the same way as our very distant ancestors?

Granted, some clothing and tech retailers now request an email address in order to electronically send receipts, but even this is a somewhat cumbersome solution (as anyone who has patiently stood in line behind a customer laboriously spelling out their name will attest). However, there are now serious moves towards digitizing the record of everything we buy.

At this point you may be thinking: so what? Who needs an online reminder of our sales splurges? Sometimes they are best quietly forgotten about, right? Well, no, not really. Receipts are handy for a number of reasons. First, they are a step in gaining incredibly useful clarity on what you are spending and where, which will in turn give you a head start in gaining greater control over your money. If, for example, you have an accessible readout that shows you are routinely spending £15 a week at an artisan coffee shop, yet you can barely make it through the month on your salary, it may be time to make adjustments. Additionally, if receipts are issued electronically, it reduces waste, since paper receipts will no longer be required. That means savings on paper, oil and water: all components used in receipts. If you are worried about the environment, this will help you do your bit. Plus, if the process is digitized, it should have an effect on reducing the time spent at the checkout.

Another advantage that is well worth flagging up is the increased security presented by the move towards digital receipts. A detailed paper trail, with documented proof of purchases, means it is far easier for banks, retailers and customers to unravel any disputed transactions if anything goes awry.

Best for: seamless integration with banking app

Receipts are notoriously difficult to keep track of, which rather negates their purpose of being a meaningful record of a sale. Apps such as *Flux* and *Sensibill* change this situation entirely and have the power to store, summarize and analyse receipts, seamlessly integrating what we spend, where we spend it and how. Using AI, they make it possible to 'read' receipts like humans do (if they took them out of the carrier bag, that is), when you pay for your goods. The app understands every data point of the receipt, categorizes them and assigns them to separate budgets within your banking app.

Flux is currently partnered with *Starling*, *Barclays* and *Monzo*, while *Sensibill* is working with banks such as *RBS* and *NatWest*. As a customer, all you need to do is to switch it on and pay for your goods as normal. The app then creates a data exchange between the retailer you shop with and your bank, when you pay with your card. The app will log the itemized transaction from the shop's point-of-sale system and collate it within the banking app. You will then not only see the full value of the total transaction but also a full list of what you've bought. Rather than, say, a debit of £5 to Costa, you'll know that you had a soy latte and an almond croissant. (So much for those good intentions.)

Digital receipts are another breakthrough that has been developed thanks to open banking. Rather than trying to build a completely new device that attempts to convince customers to pay in a different way, fintechs like *Flux* and *Sensibill* have worked with banks and retailers and built on their existing infrastructure.

Apps for that: *Flux*, *Sensibill*

Notes

1 Deloitte [accessed 26 July 2017] Customer loyalty: A relationship, not just a scheme [Online] www2.deloitte.com/content/dam/Deloitte/uk/Documents/consumer-business/deloitte-uk-consumer-review-customer-loyalty.pdf
2 Cashback Industry Report [accessed 21 September 2015] A global industry comes of age [Online] www.cashbackindustryreport.com

CHAPTER SIX

Maximize savings and investments

From self-driving cars, to online ordering, to voice-controlled super-assistants, machines are already a growing part of our lives. Computers have been making everything faster and smarter in almost everything we do for a while now. This includes making it a lot easier and quicker to spend our money anywhere, anytime. You may well remember the first occasion you used a service like PayPal to buy something online and the pleasant surprise of not needing to laboriously input a wealth of personal data. We've now got plenty of other fast and simple payment options to choose from, such as ApplePay and Google Wallet.

With our spending habits abundantly catered for, what then of our savings? How is technology helping us put money by for a rainy day? And, better still, helping our nest eggs grow into a useful amount? Not everyone feels capable of dealing effectively with their own finances, so how can technology help?

The answer is: in a lot of very interesting ways. In fact, there are two key advances that are at play here, both of which are having a big impact on savings and investments. The first is *machine learning*, which is the business of prediction. Machine learning is what helps businesses anticipate what we are going to do next by drawing on our past behaviour. Once they've got a pretty good idea of what we're likely to do, it is possible to make helpful recommendations of what we might need to achieve it. Machine learning predictions are pretty accurate too, and accuracy is good when it comes to the cash in our pockets.

The second factor that is having an impact is AI. The beauty of AI is that it cuts out the need to have a real live person reacting and making decisions on our behalf. Human interaction is fantastic, but, let's face it, we are sometimes slow. However hard we try or however well-trained we are, we do get things wrong now and again. More pertinently, we are subject to biases and emotions that affect our decision-making abilities. AI guarantees quick and objective decisions and, since the best financial decisions are taken objectively, this can only be a good thing.

What does this all mean to you and me and our personal finances? Well, machine learning and AI have the capability to quickly crunch through vast swathes of data. In other words, this technology can gather, interpret and make sense of data at a rate far exceeding what can be done by you or me. This hyper-efficient use of data makes for increasingly personalized and intelligent recommendations that will help us manage and build our wealth. Sure, the machines haven't yet reached a level of 'general' intelligence on a par with the human brain (this branch of AI is known as super intelligent AI), but when it comes to making numerical calculations, predictions and recommendations, they can't be beaten.

Machine learning is already playing a significant role in saving and budgeting. Apps are able to gather our data, work out exactly what we are earning and spending, and make informed recommendations on how to allocate our funds differently. The aim is that no money will go to waste or be spent with little or no thought. With this sort of machine-led scrutiny, it is much easier to see the things we inadvertently do that are wrecking our finances. It can be used to help give us a nudge in the right direction so there are no nasty surprises.

Meanwhile, AI is making it easier for us to do mundane tasks such as planning for bills and making sure we have enough funds to pay them on time. It also enables us to juggle between various online accounts so we know our true financial situation at any one time. You never know, you may actually have more money than you thought. With technology like this everything becomes more convenient and, just as importantly, nothing gets overlooked.

Most people don't feel the need for full-blown financial advice. There may simply be a requirement for some basic planning in weighing up whether to put money aside for savings, or pay off debts. However, individuals with higher amounts of savings, investments or earnings may feel they'd benefit from speaking to an adviser. Of course, the days when you could actually talk to someone at a bank to explain your own individual situation and receive bespoke advice about how to make the most out of your money, are long gone. With one-to-one attention becoming increasingly elusive over recent years, people have been left to muddle along as best they can. Although banks are very well aware that this is the best service a financial organization can possibly give to its customers, unfortunately it is also the most expensive way of dealing with them. This is why advisers, and indeed the branches they used to work out of, have been disappearing at a tremendous rate. Meanwhile, signing up an independent financial adviser (IFA) can seem like a daunting prospect. Although tougher regulations have been introduced (such as the Retail Distribution Review, brought into effect in 2013 by the Financial Conduct Authority as part of its consumer protection strategy) forcing regulated advisers to hold higher levels of qualifications and banning commission on the sales of financial products, the quality of advice can vary and the charges can often be difficult to fathom.

Fortunately, the days of not speaking to a financial expert from one year to the next are now behind us. Thanks to AI-driven personal assistants, or 'robo-advisers', advanced AI algorithms can make intelligent, bespoke recommendations to individuals about anything from investments to savings accounts. Those active recommendations are entirely tailored to you and you alone, based on your personal data. Each time you communicate with your bank or investment service provider, AI is able to learn something else about you and can use that information to give informed advice. There is no longer any need for a one-size-fits-all approach, or for products sold on the basis that they suit the financial institution selling them, rather than the customer. You'll always get the best solution that suits your immediate and long-term needs. If you have specific queries, your robo-adviser will be able to deal with them.

Are there downsides? After all, we are still social animals. It doesn't matter how fancy the digital world becomes, or what extraordinary products it manages to develop, we will always crave some sort of human interaction. We want to think that whoever or whatever we converse with 'gets' us as individuals. Arguably though, while you will not be sitting across the table from an actual person, the partnership between machine learning and AI does offer this potential. By accurately analysing your data, financial institutions know more about you than ever before and can make sure you get the right service. In fact, it could very well be the catalyst to rebuild our love-hate relationship with the financial services industry.

In the section that follows I have listed just some of the ways both machine learning and AI will change the way you interact with the financial world and how it will transform the way you save and invest.

Get control over your spending: employ a digital CFO

Making rational decisions about our money is not always easy. We are bombarded with tempting choices about things to buy all day, every day. Everyone wants your cash. It may be a cut price offer that catches your eye, a fantastic new (must have!) product, or you'll become distracted by a smooth-tongued sales person who convinces you that you absolutely, positively, have to have

X, Y or Z. It's not just a case of you being weak willed and spend-thrift either. Retailers spend hundreds of thousands of pounds on advertising and marketing and even perfect their store layouts so you are guaranteed to pass by something that will catch your eye. Sometimes you'll be able to resist, but sooner or later we nearly all give in to temptation. It is often not until a few days later that we start to feel regret, especially if our purchase pushes us into a situation where there is now more month left than money. And that's when it all starts to unravel. When good intentions go out the window, it doesn't take long to get into debt. One small mistake can quickly send finances spiralling out of control and see bank overdraft charges adding up.

Once upon a time, the only person who ever really bothered about a deteriorating financial situation like this was YOU. The onus has been on us, as individuals, to take responsibility for keeping track of our monthly incomings and outgoings. Banks weren't really all that bothered, as if anyone lets things get out of hand, they are the beneficiaries of sky-high overdraft charges. The Financial Conduct Authority in the UK has proposed reforms for the British market where the price for each overdraft should be a simple, single interest rate, rather than an apparently arbitrary figure, but at the time of writing this is still at the review stage. Unarranged overdrafts are still a very costly way of getting credit. However, despite that ever-present threat of charges, keeping track of things by yourself isn't always easy to do though, particularly when trying to do an oh-so-quick mental calculation when standing in front of the object of your desire. (Can I afford that pair of shoes/coat/ticket? It is a week and a half to pay day and I do have the house insurance to pay this month...) Hardly surprisingly, when the pressure is on, the numbers don't always add up and mistakes are made.

It's not just dodgy maths that gets many of us into trouble. Many people are just *too scared* to scrutinize their true financial situation. According to research, 4 in 10 adults have little or no understanding of their present financial position,[1] two-thirds couldn't say accurately what is in their bank account, while 64 per cent can't give an exact figure of what they owe on credit cards. It's not just 'ordinary' people that don't completely understand the full situation either. I once had a very illuminating conversation with a financial journalist who told me that she thought paying 1p per £7 of overdraft was no big deal. She even used the word 'cheap'. I had to explain that this could work out at £1 per day per £700 of overdraft, or £30 a month if the account holder was permanently overdrawn.

Many banks make a great deal of noise about innovative overdraft charge structures and daily flat fees. But these can be pretty costly too. If, for example, your overdraft has a 50p per day charge and you are overdrawn by £100 for 31 days, you'll be charged £15.50.

It really doesn't help that there is a multiplicity of charging structures for going overdrawn. It means that the chances are you are relying on guesswork as to what you have available to pay off bills each month, or how long it will take to clear the balance on credit cards. No wonder things sometimes unravel.

Imagine then if you had a readily available source that could give you an instant reckoning on what you do or don't have available to spend. Something that could say the equivalent of, *go on treat yourself, it's fine*. Or, alternatively, warn you, *don't buy that now. Wait until next month*. And of course, you do: your mobile phone. Many of the latest mobile banking apps give such a detailed breakdown of what is coming in and where it is all going (or going to go in the near future) that it is like having a digital CFO in your pocket. For those unfamiliar with company hierarchies, CFO stands for Chief Financial Officer. CFOs are employed by large organizations to manage a company's finances, including financial planning, managing any risks to the company coffers, keeping accurate records and reporting the annual figures. They are absolute experts in budget management, cost-benefit analysis and in forecasting any future demands, money-wise. They are exactly the type of people you need to have around when you want to keep things 100 per cent on track financially.

For nearly everyone, no two months are ever the same. Here again, your digital CFO can come to the fore. Once all your details are known, it will anticipate expenses you may have forgotten about. It also understands that not all expenses fit into a month-by-month time frame. You may, for example, be paid fortnightly or weekly, rather than once a month. Or even more sporadically, if you are part of today's gig economy. You may have certain recurring expenses that occur more or less often than monthly. Again, leave it to your digital CFO to iron out the wrinkles and create a clearer snapshot of what you really have to spend, right now.

Best for: full, real-time insights into day-to-day spending

Used to the full, your mobile money app can be your own personal digital CFO. Features available today on banking apps go way beyond the ability to simply check balances and transfer cash between accounts. The most advanced versions itemize income and expenses so you can easily track your spending habits. They list all your sources of income versus your monthly expenditures and use easy-to-understand graphics to break them down into required expenses such as rent or mortgage payments, or monthly groceries, and discretionary spending, such as eating out or clothes shopping. There is, at a glance, an instant, accurate picture of your personal cash flow.

At Starling Bank, as well as app-based institutions, real-time payment notifications are an ever-present visual reminder: there is no way to avoid the reality of what you are spending on a day-to-day basis. You'll get insights into your everyday spending habits and will easily see how much you spent in a particular shop. It can sting a bit at first, especially for anyone who has long avoided knowing their true cash position, but it is a lot easier to keep things in check when you have a detailed idea of your finances. Other apps with similar features include *Monzo*, *Revolut* and *N26*.

If you find you are consistently spending more than you are bringing in each month, go to your expenses snapshot and let your digital CFO show you where you are allocating your money and what areas you could possibly adjust to make up the difference. If, on the other hand, you consistently have money spare each month, you can work out what to do with the extra.

Don't just idly muse: can I afford it? Find out! Ask your very own digital CFO.

Apps for that: *Starling, Monzo, Revolut, N26*

Best for: active intervention to prevent overspending

Most good budgeting apps take a 'dashboard' approach, enabling you to hook up all your account info into one place, so you can accurately see what is going in and out. It's even possible to play around with the figures to see how you could improve your situation without making too much of a change to your lifestyle. *Money Dashboard* has pie charts and graphs that can be adjusted so you can see exactly how much you could save each year if, say, you got out of bed 20 minutes earlier each day and made yourself a takeaway Americano and a packed lunch. It's a read-only tool, so you can't move money around to help make these changes, but it is a useful visual reminder of how to improve your day-to-day situation. *Yolt* is another alternative that links data from your current accounts, savings accounts and credit cards, so you can check all your transactions and balances in the same place. The graphics are good and help to get a good visual snapshot of your monthly position. The best feature is a 'smart balance' that shows how much of the total across your accounts needs to go on bills and essentials, and how much is left for more enjoyable pursuits.

For a more hands-on intervention by your digital CFO, you may turn to *Squirrel*, which practises a bit more of a tough love approach. To use it, you'll need to hold an account with Barclays. Pay in your salary and then the app releases money gradually into your current account so you don't splurge. The weekly allowance can be set to your liking (or at least to what you can afford), and it also ensures bills are paid and holds back money each month for savings. The app is really useful for anyone who struggles to stay out of the overdraft zone.

Meanwhile, *Cleo* is a chatbot assistant with read-only access to your accounts who will give instant answers to questions about spending and savings, so you can pause and take a deep breath before doing something you may later regret. If you've ever shouted: 'where has it all gone', while staring in horror at your balance, this may be the app for you. It'll tell you exactly where you've spent it all.

Apps for that: *Money Dashboard, Yolt, Squirrel, Cleo*

Best for: joint accounts

They say opposites attract, but if you are super frugal and your partner is prone to wild spending sprees, you have just cause to reconsider pooling your finances in a joint account. Or, at the very least, you may like to keep a very close eye on exactly what is being spent in that account. *Starling* offers a joint account, with the same easy set up as its individual accounts. It is really handy because it is a great way to see both of your account balances in one place. There are also other apps to consider such as *Money Dashboard, Spendee* and *Mint*. Once each account is linked to the app, transaction types can be grouped and categorized so you have a clearer view of what is being spent and where. It's the perfect way to be completely transparent on what you are spending, and the overview across multiple accounts is a really helpful feature. It'll also ensure you have better, more informed, conversations about money. You don't necessarily need to be in an intimate relationship with the person you are sharing details with. Shared wallets via the apps can be a really helpful way of managing budgets between, say, flatmates.

Once you both know exactly, in real time, where everything is going, you'll be able to make better, more informed financial decisions about the future.

Apps for that: *Starling, Money Dashboard, Spendee, Mint*

Saving for a specific goal

If you'll forgive the extension of the digital CFO metaphor, it is worth mentioning that, in business, CFOs serve a dual role. Not only do they manage a firm's day-to-day finance needs, keeping records and providing detailed analyses of figures, but they also play an important part in future forecasting. In other words, they make sure a business always has adequate funds to achieve what it needs to achieve and is never thrown off course by any sudden surprises. They also plan ahead for any significant investments a company might like to make in the months and years ahead. All of this, inevitably, requires that adequate cash be put to one side.

Once again, this is exactly the sort of service you should be expecting from your very own digital CFO. One of the many useful features in the mobile bank apps listed in the previous section is a facility that calculates how much you can afford to save each week. Money is then automatically 'swept' into a separate savings account.

Whether it is university fees, a new home, or a dream holiday, everyone has a milestone in their mind's eye. And these significant items usually take a great deal of cash. Short of selling something valuable to pay for it (and there is only so much you can sell to raise money), the only way to achieve the sum required is saving. Regularly.

Savings are not just all about big dreams of treating yourself one day in the future either. Ideally, we should all have a cushion of at least three months' salary to protect against the unexpected, but in reality, very few people do. Yet, even setting aside an emergency fund of a few hundred pounds would be a big help if you are suddenly faced with an unplanned for bill. However, you need to be disciplined to build up that emergency fund.

Small steps can and do lead to big changes. In other words, apps that assist you in getting into healthy savings habits will help to begin transforming your future outlook. In fact, this is where app-based technology comes into its own. Enter a target amount and a deadline and let the app set a savings schedule, showing how much you'll need to keep putting aside each month.

Best for: visualizing savings progress

A number of savings apps take a lead from the old-fashioned jam jar approach to saving money. This was where, in years gone by, households would literally divide up their budgets into weekly piles, with one for rent, one for food, one for a rainy day and so on. *Starling* has 'Goals', which is a digital version of these jam jars where you can stash away the amount you'd like to save whenever you like. It's possible to visualize objectives by adding your own image to the goal 'jar' of, say, the golden sands of the beach outside your coveted Caribbean getaway, or of that nifty little sports car you've always coveted.

There are other, dedicated jam jar style apps too, such as *Goodbudget* and *Mvelopes*, both of which link accounts, categorize spending and assign transactions to dedicated zones for safekeeping. With the *Savings Goals* app, users can enter a target amount for any long-term savings project, along with a deadline by which they want to have the full amount. The app calculates a savings schedule of how much you need to put by each month or week and then tracks your progress. You can also set it to round up day-to-day transactions to the nearest pound and sweep the extra amount into a goal of your choice. Set the round up to multiply 2x, 5x, or 10x to accelerate the savings process.

It's easy to tell any of these apps to save less one month if you are up against it (although it is not advised to make a habit of it), or to move money back into your current account if a truly unexpected expense looms large.

Apps for that: *Goodbudget, Mvelopes, Savings Goals*

Best for: allocating spare funds when available

If you simply can't afford to squirrel away significant amounts every month, don't worry. Even small amounts will eventually add up. Automatic savings accounts such as *Chip* and *Plum* work out how much you can afford to save without it having a massive impact on your usual spending habits. They need to be linked to your current account, but only for read-only access to see your transactions. *Plum* works with Facebook, whereas *Chip* works as its own app. Every few days algorithms calculate whether or not there is any spare capacity, however little, and then transfers the money automatically to your account. With *Chip*, 1 per cent interest is offered as standard, but you can boost that by anything from another 1 per cent to a maximum of 5 per cent if you recommend friends to sign up too. If you are having a flush week, it is also possible to manually add to your *Chip* pot. The interest rates are pretty generous at the time of writing, as the app seeks to build up customers, but investments are subject to a daily cap of £100.

Apps for that: *Chip, Plum*

Best for: keeping track

Of course, there is another side to saving money, which is, well, saving money. By this I mean, not wasting it, or losing track of it. Getting on top of your cash flow means that, even if you enjoy being the most generous soul in your crowd, you need to ensure you don't get yourself into trouble because you lose sight of who owes you cash.

It's an easy thing to do when you're splitting a restaurant bill, or chipping in for a friend's birthday present, or taking care of a communal food shop. You pay the full amount to make things easier and the next thing you know you are left with the headache of reconciling the account. There are digital solutions to this age-old problem. *Splitwise* is an app where you can create groups with various friends and divide up what each person owes. Everyone's expenses and IOUs are logged in one place so each person in the group can see what they owe everyone else. The app tracks all the borrowing and lending between you over time and sends out reminders at the end of each month so everyone can pay anything outstanding and start the new month afresh. Payments can be settled via PayPal or cash, in which case the settlement can be manually logged in the app.

FlyPay is a big help when restaurants present a large group with a bill. You can order your food through the app and it automatically divides up the bill so everyone knows who pays what. It also lets you pay through the app in venues such as Gourmet Burger Kitchen, Jamie's Italian and Wahaca, saving you having to flag down a waiter. Just pay and then get up and leave.

Finally, not to forget *Starling Settle Up* and *Monzo Me*, which are built into the banking apps to make it easier for friends and family to request and receive payments from each other. The process means that there are no sort codes to swap, or details to double check, just a few taps and you've settled up.

Apps for that: *Splitwise, FlyPay*

Note

1 Newcastle Building Society [accessed 9 May 2016] Attitudes to money [Online] www.newcastle.co.uk

CHAPTER SEVEN

Pay-as-you-go insurance

Let's face it. The greatest problem with insurance is no one ever really wants to buy it. Sure, we all know that we *need* it, or that it is a *wise* investment, or that it is even *compulsory* in some instances such as driving, but it doesn't mean it's a purchase any of us enjoys or particularly welcomes. This widespread ambivalence could partly be the reason why, until now, the insurance industry has been somewhat slow to innovate. Certainly, the various forms of insurance have garnered far less attention from would-be disruptors than other finance sectors that have enjoyed some tremendous fintech advances. Yes, apps have appeared that promise to make the experience of choosing an insurance provider faster or easier, or that have enabled us to shop around various insurers, but there has been little rush to try to unlock the widespread apathy about buying insurance.

There's another potential barrier to anyone considering the disruptive route too. The industry already has challenges of its own when it comes to bringing out exciting new products to shake up the somewhat slow-moving world of insurance.

Aside from the large number of government regulations covering this sector, the possible outcomes it needs to cover are also notoriously unpredictable (which is why we need insurance!). 'Acts of God' from tsunamis, to wildfires, to earthquakes, to floods, to common-or-garden road traffic accidents, all make the business hard to read. Like it or not, a lot falls outside data norms.

Nevertheless, today, there is no shortage of businesses beginning to wake up to the potential for the insurance market and having a very good go at revolutionizing this very traditional business. In fact, so much money has been poured into the sector, it has spawned its own buzzword: insurtech. It's like fintech, but for the insurance industry.

Something that is already proving to be quite effective for the burgeoning insurtech industry is the widespread and constantly growing demand for ever more personalized goods and services. Whatever it is we are buying, we all want to know we are getting what we pay for and that we are getting the right product for us as individuals. As discussed at the beginning of this book, the Internet of Things and our super-connected world means that bespoke products and services are now becoming increasingly possible in all walks of life. And, that includes insurance. Insurers now have the capacity to vary premiums according to our own, unique circumstances. We have already seen evidence of this with the introduction of car insurance that can be bought by the journey. It is also possible to secure discounts on our motor insurance premiums by installing a telematics device to track how safely we are driving. This has been a huge bonus for young drivers who may otherwise not be able to afford to get out onto the road. Elsewhere, some health insurance providers are offering gym fee reimbursements for people who wear fitness trackers.

Even so, it is early days when it comes to the disruption of insurance. We are right at the beginning of the process of exploring all the possibilities. However, now insurtechs are waking up to the potential in this market, all sorts of great ideas will inevitably begin to come to the fore. Facial recognition technology is tipped to play a role in assessing the level of cover needed for life policies, for example. After all, experts (and indeed computers) can already tell a huge range of things about us and our lifestyles by 'reading' our faces. It seems our appearance can provide as much information on our age, lifestyle, health and smoking habits as any 10-page questionnaire.

Data gathered from the Internet of Things and biometrics is the tip of the iceberg. Insurers are becoming ever more willing to embrace lifestyle apps that enable them to gather data about us in order to give more accurate quotes. This should be good news for all of us. Now insurers are receiving more detailed information about where the true risks lie, their pricing should become keener too.

Reinventing insurance is not an easy task and, like I say, we are right at the beginning of a process of innovative thinking. In this chapter, I've covered some of the most interesting start-ups and developments around right now.

Reinvention of the insurance model

Without a doubt, one of the biggest challenges that has blighted the insurance sector in recent years is trust. On both sides.

In the truest sense of the word, insurance is supposed to be about the pooling of shared risk between insurer and insured. Somehow though, over time, that ideal has lost its way and the business model has evolved into one that is all about the insured and the insurer both chasing the same pot of money. That was never going to work well and, hardly surprisingly, it has led to a situation where whenever a claim is made, one or both sides feel aggrieved or that the other side has not lived up to the terms of the original agreement.

How did this happen? Historically, insurers have had to shoulder very large overheads, thanks to a high cost-of-sales and heavy administrative costs. This led the industry to collectively do its best to *minimize* the amount it paid out in claims. Before long, insurance companies gained a reputation for being quick to throw out anything that fell even vaguely outside of the terms of the agreement. Worse still, it even saw occasional refusals to pay out on entirely legitimate claims. Not surprisingly, this state of affairs prompted an erosion of trust between insurers and the insured. We've now reached a situation where everyone expects their insurers to automatically try to chip away at the amount of a pay-out or even refuse altogether, when push comes to shove.

Most paying customers naturally resent being put into the position of believing they have to jump through hoops to prove their innocence before receiving a penny. It has therefore not been unknown for people to try to 'pre-empt' the potential for their claim to be whittled down by lumping a few extra items into it. In a burglary, for example, they may list things that were not really lost or stolen at all, alongside valuables that had been taken. The thinking seems to go: if they add on a bit and the insurer takes away a bit, it'll somehow balance up alright in the end. Inevitably a bit of back and forth will ensue that will no doubt further drive up the insurer's administrative costs and further perpetuate the problem. Sometimes the consumer wins, but mostly the insurer does. Either way, the process doesn't do anyone any good and things only get worse. The net result is most people hold a pretty low opinion of the insurance industry and do their best to spend as little time thinking about it, or interacting with it, as possible.

For a long while it was believed that no amount of exciting tech could solve this fundamental imbalance between consumer expectations and the insurance business model. As with all industries that come under the gaze of disruptors, the solution is to take drastic action. Insurtech innovators have decided that, rather than wasting time trying to digitize traditional insurance, they need to change the model completely, building entirely new insurance products that operate in a completely different way. The biggest irony of all is that the basis of the new approach nods to the earliest idea of pooling shared risk, bringing the insurance business full circle. Thanks to this new thinking (or revival of old thinking) we are already seeing some very innovative solutions to the trust issue.

Under a peer-to-peer system, or P2P as it is known, the group of insured is far smaller. It can even be a group of close friends or family who pool their resources to provide support in the event that one or more of them suffers some sort of misfortune. If the period of coverage ends without incident, premiums can be returned to everyone in the pool.

Best for: pooling the risk

US-based insurance app *Lemonade* has eliminated the trust issue by ensuring it doesn't make any gain from the non-payment of claims. They charge a flat fee, taking a 20 per cent cut from monthly policy payments. Key to the way the app operates is a 'giveback' scheme, where any unclaimed money is given to good causes. The way it works is this: customers select a charity they care about through the app and then all users who select the same cause are put into a group. Premiums that are paid into each virtual group are used to cover any subsequent claims by individuals within that same group. Any money left over at the end of the year is donated to the cause that everyone in the group opted to support. Because trust works both ways, users of the app are expected to be less likely to embellish their claims, since they won't be simply taking money from 'fat cat' insurers, rather they'll actually be reducing support to their chosen good cause. Since it is all more straightforward, *Lemonade* also promises to make payments in super-fast time.

The concept of sharing the risk among peers is taking off elsewhere too. *Friendsurance* uses social media to link friends together to buy collective polices from established insurers. Whenever anyone signs up, they join a group they already know and pay an upfront premium. If no one claims at the end of the term, everyone gets reimbursed. The service claims to receive between 20 per cent to 40 per cent less claims than conventional insurers. The idea perfectly mimics the old concept of mutual insurance where people are encouraged to look after their own needs and risks through shared responsibility.

Apps for that: *Lemonade, Friendsurance*

Best for: social insurance

Teambrella markets itself as being a tool that not only eliminates the need for an insurer but also eliminates risk because everyone's interests are aligned. Customers are formed into teams of self-governing user communities with the scope to approve or deny claims with the app, which is currently being piloted in six countries, including the United States, Germany and the Netherlands. The members of each *Teambrella* 'team' are responsible for covering each other and decide everything from a person's risk profile, to how much they are covered for, to the legitimacy of their claim. It's all out in the open too, for everyone to comment upon. Once the level of the premium has been agreed by the team, each team member puts their 'premium' into a digital wallet. It's rather like an escrow account (a third party account that holds cash during a transaction). The sum remains in the digital wallet and can be called upon if anyone else on the team makes a claim that is then approved by the other team members. If no claims are made, then the money stays in the digital wallet.

A UK firm, *So-Sure* markets another form of 'social insurance'. Here groups of friends can insure their phones and online portals together. The best bit? You get 80 per cent of your money back, every year, as long as no one in the group breaks, loses or has their phone stolen. What's great about this is that getting your money back is purely dependent on your friends not claiming, not on the claims of anyone you don't know. The risk/reward is only shared with the people you know and trust.

All of these new insurance products perfectly tap into the idea of a sharing economy. Peer-to-peer, or group-pooling models like this hold out the promise of transparency and fairness in handling claims, potentially injecting a much-needed air of trust into this industry.

Apps for that: *Teambrella, So-Sure*

The connected home

When it comes to home insurance, the latest thinking favours a shift away from the idea of a property being simply *insured*, to one where our houses and possessions are permanently *protected*. In other words, the goal is to predict and prevent, rather than repair and replace. Once again, the Internet of Things plays a huge role here. Smart sensors around the home can be deployed to collect data on everything from temperature, to water and electricity consumption, to a possible intruder, so the home-owner can be alerted if anything is wrong and can intervene before any damage can be done.

These predict and prevent models hold out the enticing prospect of far more accurate (and potentially cheaper) premiums too. Instead of every household in the same street being presented with the same insurance quote, there's an opportunity to tailor quotes to individual situations, which is far fairer. Data collected from smart homes is highly personalized and can be collated and compared to get more competitive quotes. As the tech improves the premiums should get ever more accurate and, hopefully, less expensive.

Best for: smart home insurance

The *Neos* app encourages customers to create their own smart home by installing a range of internet-connected sensors, all of which are included in the price of the insurance. The app then monitors and manages the various sensors and can even control some of the components they are attached to, whether they be motion sensors, cameras or smoke detectors. Everything in a smart home is, of course, linked to a customer's phone. Thus, if the front door is left open, or a leak sprouts beneath the kitchen sink (leaks are the biggest source of home insurance claims, accounting for about a third[1]), it lets the customer know, so they can do something about it before it becomes an issue. In a neat bit of connective thinking, the app also aims to connect customers with repair services, so everything is easily to hand should the worst happen. It even keeps a log of trusted keyholders who can let a plumber in if the homeowner is away.

Neos is not the only insurance business making a move this way. Established insurers and start-ups alike are viewing 'smart' home insurance as the way forward and developing products that closely monitor what goes on in our homes. The challenge will be to get households to buy into the idea and connect up their homes. It is highly likely that, in the short term at least, many companies will need to start off by offering some sort of discount to help homeowners install the tech they need. *PolicyCastle*, another home insurance start-up, already offers customers a 15 per cent discount if they install an approved smart home security system or leak detector. If equipment is already installed, customers can upload photographs of the equipment to the app and if the customer subsequently adds the systems to their home mid-way through the policy, the premium can be adjusted.

Apps for that: *Neos, PolicyCastle*

Best for: fast renewals

Another benefit from the increased quantities of data being gathered via smart devices is that home insurance is becoming easier to renew. Like so many forms of insurance, setting up a home policy has traditionally required completing an extensive questionnaire before a rate for the cover can be set and the policy agreed. With more data being kept on record, this process should speed up considerably. Indeed, reduced bureaucracy is another aspect of home insurance being tackled by insurtech firms. *Homelyfe* is an app that promises households they can find and buy cover in under four minutes. It is also working with third parties so other apps, such as mobile banks, can offer their customers insurance cover without them ever having to leave the original banking app to set it up.

App for that: *Homelyfe*

Best for: renters

Another neat idea in the housing insurance market that is well worth mentioning here are developments in deposit replacement insurance schemes. This is something that the rental market has been crying out for, for years. As any renter will attest, finding a deposit before you can secure a rental and move in is often as difficult as finding a property to rent in the first place. Add on the letting agent's fees and the resulting large bill can present a very big challenge indeed for renters. Then, just to make things that little bit harder, if you are moving from one rented property to the next, you'll often need to find the fresh deposit before you get the one back from your previous rental.

There are now insurance policies to cover this side of things and cut out the need to scrabble around to find a deposit, which can add up to the equivalent of several weeks' rent payments. The thinking behind policies from *Dlighted* and *Canopy* is to indemnify the risk of tenant damage or unpaid rent. *Dlighted* is paid by the landlord or letting agent, not the renter. At the end of the rental period, disputes are initially resolved with the tenant, but if an agreement is not reached, the landlord or agent can make a claim, with the tenant liable for the cost of the claim. *Canopy* works in the opposite way, where the tenant pays for the policy. *Canopy* promises to empower renters and enables them to pay for deposit insurance via a web app or smart phone. It uses a 'RentPassport' to hold information about the renter's credit and rental history. The services provide landlords with the same cover as a cash security deposit, with the tenant retaining responsibility for any loss or damage or unpaid rent at the end of the rental.

This sort of insurance is great for anyone who struggles to find a deposit. Obviously, if you are able to pay the initial sum easily, it's up to you to weigh up is if it is worth it to you to pay a smaller sum initially by taking the insurance, particularly since it is also money you'll never get back. If you are the sort of person who usually meets all your obligations, rental wise, you may be better off with the old system.

Apps for that: *Dlighted*, *Canopy*

Life insurance for the life you lead

Social media has been a huge bonus for insurance companies. In fact, our willingness to publicly post anything and everything about our daily lives has proved to be invaluable. Insurance giants have large departments dedicated to trawling through endless cute kitten or dancing baby posts. Why? Because when they spot an online boast that someone has just completed a 10K run, it can be pretty illuminating, especially if that same breathless poster has also made a large claim for compensation because they are 'practically housebound'.

That's an extreme example, but the social media investigative departments of insurance companies have become a crucial tool when it comes to assisting with claims and catching out fraud. It's all perfectly legal too. Read the fine print on your social media platforms and the T&Cs clearly state that if material is posted online it can be picked up by investigators and used against you if you've done anything illegal. If you are still surprised that they have the ability to do this, don't be. It is nothing new or unusual. 'Big Brother' is watching you all the time via online behavioural tracking techniques. You have surely noticed that after whiling away a pleasant morning searching Google for a suitable new sofa, you are subsequently inundated with pop-up home furnishings ads for the next few weeks? Nothing we do these days stays private for very long.

Of course, since it is happening anyhow, you might take the view that we all may as well reap the positives from the development. And there are positives, even in insurance. The next step in the connected world we now live in is for the providers of life insurance to use what you freely lay bare about your lifestyle online to produce more accurately tailored quotes that reflect the life you lead. In other words, instead of your personal information being used against you, it can now actually be used to help you secure more accurate and cost-effective life insurance premiums.

Reading this, your first reaction may be one of horror. You may think: *Why would I want anyone looking into my intimate details? My social media feed is for friends and family, not strangers.* You'd not be alone. One of the greatest challenges the life insurance industry has always faced is that it has been difficult to even get customers to the point where they are willing to sign off on letting an insurer look more closely into their social media posts. Aside from the issue of privacy, most people simply don't believe they need that level of scrutiny. In actual fact, most people don't even like to think they'll require life insurance protection at all. After all, who wants to consider that something bad might happen to them? Sadly, it does happen and more often than most of us would care to know. In fact, 1 child in 29 loses a parent before they become adults themselves. The shock of this event is often compounded by the corresponding loss of income, which can send the rest of the family spiralling into financial crisis.

Now, if you still don't like the idea of strangers snooping through your posts about your party lifestyle, don't worry. This development is another of those that you *opt into*, open banking style. Once you give the go ahead to individual apps they will be able to use your online life to gather more information about you. They may view LinkedIn data for a pretty good idea of your income bracket, Facebook for an indicator of how much you enjoy risk and so on. Insurers such as *Hiscox*, *QBE* and *MetLife* are already using data like this to give more individualized product recommendations to customers.

Best for: easy application process

The insurtech industry is now focussed on finding the exact right way to start the conversation about life insurance, so more people are better protected. The latest thinking is to use technology to seamlessly introduce the possibility at exactly the right moment. This might be, for example, following the birth of a baby or when buying a house. The new generation of products from apps such as *Anorak*, which bills itself as a 'smart' life insurance adviser, involves partnering with third parties, such as mobile banks, price comparison websites, or brokers, to make the application relevant and simple, with the minimum amount of 'form filling'. *Anorak* uses data science to process relevant data about a person's home, family, income and finances to assess the type of cover needed. The technology then scans and rates policies from most major insurers to deliver completely bespoke advice in minutes. It also prides itself on 'translating' insurance jargon into plain English.

App for that: *Anorak*

Best for: customizing your policy

Sherpa is an app that prides itself on letting customers chose terms that work for them. The subscriptions-based model provides all-risks personal cover and invites those being insured to dial their required level of cover up or down, which can then be subsequently changed as needs or circumstances alter. Here, customers effectively join a club, paying a membership fee for access to insurance cover. It effectively makes *Sherpa* their digital insurance adviser, which assesses all aspects of the customer's lifestyle to work out the right cover. *Sherpa* then packages up insurance needs from multiple customers and buys cover wholesale from reinsurers.

App for that: *Sherpa*

Drive smart

We've already touched upon one of the biggest developments in car insurance in the first part of this book: the advent of just-in-time or pay-as-you-go apps such as *Cuvva* and *By Miles*. The idea perfectly taps into the developments in data technology that make it very easy to track and trace everything we do and therefore only pay for the services we use.

Of course, the big change in the car market all insurtechs are anticipating is the launch of fully automated, driverless cars, which will transform the motor industry entirely. A whole new list of possible risks will come into play into the future. What, for example, would happen if there were a mass hacking event? (I know it all sounds a bit dramatic, but it's impossible to discount the risk, which is something that is no doubt focussing the minds of insurers.) Usually, car thefts or accidents are independent events, with no connection between events at different locations. In a fully connected world, this may not always remain the case. At the other end of the scale, car ownership may collapse altogether. Services like Uber may simply send an automated car to your door whenever you need to go anywhere. In this case, individual policies will become entirely redundant. The insurtechs of today and the near future are going to spend a lot of time thinking about the interaction between people and machines, and this doesn't just mean the ones with two or four wheels: we need to anticipate where digital technology will take us next.

Best for: connecting premiums to driving style

At present, telematics seem to be getting the most attention in car insurance circles. Also known as 'black box' insurance, this is where a driver agrees to have sensors in their car to record how safely they drive, what sorts of roads they drive on, what times of day and how far they go. When you sign up for a policy, a black box is installed inside the car that's named within that policy. Various measurements are taken each time you drive and are shared with the insurer. The resulting data is used to provide far more accurate insurance calculations.

Telematics policies cost the same as a normal policy initially, but insurers have the ability to adjust the premium in line with the data being collected and monitored. This is where the technology comes into its own, since drivers can monitor the data too. Once 'scores' from the monitor are known, it is possible to adjust driving styles to drive more safely to reduce premiums. People who drive erratically know they are in danger of having their premium increased, since they will be deemed more at risk of having an accident and making a claim.

Telematics insurers such as *Aviva Drive*, *Woop* and *Root* all claim telematics help to cut insurance premiums by as much as 25 per cent for safe drivers. This is particularly useful for younger drivers, who often face crippling premiums. According to research, a 17- to 24-year-old could save £363.25 by insuring in this way.[2] *Aviva Drive*'s app also has a dash cam feature so drivers can record, save and share footage in the event of a claim. Phones just have to be placed in a cradle, with the camera viewing the road ahead.

Apps for that: *Aviva Drive*, *Woop*, *Root*

Best for: watch this space!

The pooled resources, or shared economy, is another big development that is beginning to be talked about in driving apps. The idea behind it is you use money for insurance only when you have a claim. You keep your cash if you don't. The driving force behind the concept is the desire to iron out the inequality between the majority of the insured who end up paying higher premiums for the bad habits of those who drive carelessly.

Any model that is developed will be based on pooled risk, similar to the social insurance model discussed earlier, where a particular group chooses the people they want in their insurance group via their social networks. Premiums are then pooled online and, since everyone knows everyone else, they can trust them to only claim when necessary.

Also well worth keeping an eye on are digital developments in the claims process, which is always a notoriously stressful time. A Thailand-based start-up called *Claim Di* is an app that aims to smooth the way in claims between drivers and their insurance companies and can shorten the whole process. So, in the case of a minor accident, the driver can simply shake his or her phone near the phone of the other party involved and the insurance companies of both sides will issue claim reports via the *Claim Di* platform. Photos of any damage can be taken through the same app. It is even possible to search nearby for a garage or car mechanic to help you out.

Like I say, it is early days, but these are just a few examples of the innovative thinking that is making inroads into vehicle insurance (excuse the pun). Expect more disruption soon: there will be big changes in how we buy car insurance.

Master policies

Of course, to give the insurance industry the true disruptor treatment, insurtech firms need to be thinking completely differently about this somewhat staid sector altogether. And, true to form, they already are. Rather than simply adding 'tech' updates to old insurance products and putting them in a nice looking app, insurtech start-ups are starting to think about the whole proposition of insurance. Do we, for example, need one policy for our cars, one for the home and another for life insurance? Isn't there an argument for unbundling it all and starting again?

An all-in-one insurance policy makes a lot of sense from a customer point of view. You could have a relationship with just one insurer that would cover everything in one go. There would be just one renewal date a year to be mindful about and perhaps even economies of scale to be achieved. Plus, with your policies all housed with one provider, that provider will have more opportunity to learn more about you and your risk profile, and will therefore be able to offer the keenest possible price, tailored to your personal needs.

While I have laid out this chapter along the lines of the various categories of insurances you may buy, from life, to house, to car, the fact is the insurance industry has long debated whether or not we'd actually be better off just focussing on the customer, rather than the various times/applications they may need insurance to cover. This argument is more pertinent than ever in the light of new developments around the Internet of Things and the amount of data available about each and every one of us.

Obviously, I am aware that most insurance giants offer insurance policies for every conceivable situation. You could, of course, quite easily buy a series of policies from say *Arriva* or *Admiral* that cover various needs, from house, to car, to life. However, while customers may well have numerous policies from the same company, under the same name, each one would have been generated from an entirely different division of the insurer, with no cross-over whatsoever. What I am talking about here is one policy with one premium that covers each of your requirements, from one department.

Best for: early adopters

One of the earliest insurtechs to tackle this all-in-one space is German operator *Getsafe*. It started life as a digital insurance wallet, where you could keep details of all your policies in one place. It is now working towards one, single, all-encompassing policy for everything for its members (the term they use for their customers) in what is becoming known as a 'my whole life' approach. Rather similar to the *Lemonade* app described earlier, members pay a flat fee for their catch-all insurance service and any leftover premiums are given to selected charities. The *Getsafe* app helps users to understand their coverage and then customize their protection for anything from life to health insurance. This includes the ability to get add-ons with other types of insurance, or file claims via the app. Those buying insurance can customize the app to show their individual risk appetite and set excess limits as well as use it to check on exactly what is covered by the policy and what is not.

The *Getsafe* app aims to fully engage users in the traditionally somewhat-less-than-exciting world of insurance. So, for example, the dental insurance section offers reminders of routine appointments and offers incentives for members to stay healthy.

What makes all this possible is so-called digital advisers. Combining data gathering, machine learning and AI, the digital brains behind apps like *Getsafe* become a massive risk assessment tool that can take into account our individual tendencies to take high or low risks, live a sedentary or energetic life, and dozens of other factors besides. All these factors are combined to give a unique and individual view about us. This highly personalized view is gold dust for insurance companies, but it is great for you and me too.

App for that: *Getsafe*

Notes

1   Aviva [accessed 13 February 2013] Ten most common claims made against home insurance policies: list [Online] www.aviva.co.uk

2   MoneySupermarket data from quotes between January and March 2018

CHAPTER EIGHT

Pay off your mortgage

There is a reason why buying a house regularly tops polls of the most stressful life events, surpassing other gruelling milestones such as divorce, bereavement and losing a job. Dealing with solicitors, waiting for paperwork for weeks, even months, fearing that the sale could collapse at any moment and constantly chasing estate agents for updates all make for a pretty traumatic period. The void of information that amplifies a would-be home-buyer's feeling of desperation feels even worse today when set against the bountiful status alerts in nearly all other aspects of our daily lives. Delivery companies let us see the progress of our packages every step of the way, and we can even reschedule or redirect a package *en route*. Order a pizza and there'll be multiple alerts on its expected arrival time. Numerous retailers have live support links to qualified personnel who are there to help you with even the tiniest, most trivial query.

So why can't borrowers get the same sort of service from the companies they work with in order to secure what will be one of the most important purchases of their lives?

For many years, the only notable technological advances in the house-buying market centred around property portals. Yet, while search engines such as *Zoopla* and *Rightmove* certainly made the process of searching for the perfect home a lot easier, the next stage in the process of actually buying the chosen property has remained largely unchanged for decades. The mortgage market certainly appears to have remained blissfully unaware of the internet boom, bar introducing the most basic of digital facilities.

In fairness to the mortgage industry, there is a plausible argument why it hasn't been easy to move towards offering a better experience to customers. Buying a house is a remarkably complex process. There are numerous documents to review, regulations to heed and decisions that require input from all directions. If pressed, lenders would no doubt say they simply don't make enough money out of selling mortgages to justify getting in the numbers of staff that would be required to markedly improve the customer experience.

There is another reason why progress has been slow too. While nearly everyone would attest to the fact that the buying-a-home experience is one of the worst they've ever endured, the hardship is generally quickly forgotten once a homebuyer gets the keys to the front door and finds their kettle from in among their packing cases. After that, most people barely engage with their mortgage company. In fact, nearly half the population access their mortgage account less than once a year.[1] With such low engagement levels there has been little impetus for change. Put simply, no one has really complained very loudly, therefore nothing has been done.

Of course, this status quo was never going to last and certainly not in the very different, hyper-connected, extremely communicative world we find ourselves in today. The technology-enabled generation is less likely than ever to put up with lacklustre service. With every other area of our financial lives undergoing a transformation, it was unlikely mortgages would go ignored for too much longer, particularly when they consume such a high proportion of our incomes.

Things are undoubtedly beginning to happen. Mortgage providers are increasingly using technology to speed up the house sale process and smooth out any rough edges. Although progress is being made at a cautious pace, it has been predicted that the market is on the verge of mimicking much of what has gone on elsewhere in the financial sector, and things will move incrementally from now on. Fintech developments are forecast to have a huge impact on the house buying market in a range of areas. This is great news for everyone because digital ticks a lot of boxes. It's transparent, safe, secure, simple and can be tailored to an individual.

Ultimately, a mortgage is simply a means to an end; the way to help us buy the home we want. Anything that can make that process less frustrating and cumbersome, plus present the best possible choice, has to be a good thing.

Digital mortgage brokers

As a prospective home buyer will soon discover when they look closely at the mortgage market, there are a seemingly infinite number of products on offer. Yet, it is crucial not to get put off and go for the first one you find. Getting the right mortgage deal can save homeowners a massive proportion of their monthly expenditure, which can really add up over a year and especially over an entire mortgage term of 25 years.

When searching for the best mortgage deal, the best advice has always been to cast the net as widely as possible. There are many variables in the type of mortgage available, most notably with the all-important rates of interest on offer. A lot depends on the size of the deposit a home buyer is able to put down and the value of the property they want to buy.

It has traditionally been easiest to speak with a broker to get advice on what's what and recommendations as to the best mortgage for your own unique circumstance. Brokers, which can be found on the high street, through IFAs or via recommendations from estate agents, scour the market to find the best mortgage deal, giving homebuyers the benefit of a range of options from a huge number of lenders. They are also able to advise on Help to Buy mortgages and other schemes such as shared ownership.

It would be fair to assume that brokers search all available products on the market. However, this is not always the case. Some brokerage firms are limited in what they can offer. They may be tied to a particular lender or only work with a small number of them. This, of course, means they are only able to offer a limited selection of deals. Or maybe they assure you that they offer ALL the products available to brokers, with the subtle catch hidden in the last part of that assertion. Brokers may well exclude deals that lenders only offer direct to the public, mainly because they won't get any commission out of the transaction. Even if they do check lenders' direct-only deals, they may well charge a fee for this service.

Indeed, how brokers are paid for their services is another confusing part of the process. Some brokers charge a fee directly, which might be on top of the commission they earn from the lender. Alternatively, they might charge a fee and then refund the commission that is paid when the mortgage completes. They may even give homebuyers a choice between paying a fee or commission, which means they can call themselves 'independent'. Fees can also be charged during any part of the process as long as the broker clearly states this up front. In some cases, brokers can charge fees ahead of completion and then, even if the house purchase falls through, the buyer may still be liable.

On the face of it, it may seem like finding the right broker for you is almost as hard as finding the right mortgage deal! Enter the digital broker. This new breed of brokers uses cutting edge technology to search through thousands of mortgage deals. The resulting recommendation will be drawn from deals available to brokers and direct deals, with the most important criteria being finding the right one for you.

Another advantage of digital brokers is that they speed up the process, which, as well as reducing the stress and strains of home buying, is also useful in an unpredictable and competitive house market. If a would-be house buyer finds their dream home and is desperate to make an offer and get it off the market before someone else decides it is their dream home too, there has previously been an agonizing delay while a mortgage company satisfies itself that the property in question is worth the money being offered. The property is, after all, the lender's security for the loan. If the householder was subsequently unable to pay the mortgage, a lender could repossess the house and sell it to recover their money. In this sort of situation, a digital broker really comes into their own because it can instantly make the process quicker and smoother.

A great deal of the efficiency in digital brokers is down to the increased use of automated valuations (AVMs), which enable lenders to make an instant decision. This is where a valuation calculation is made based on comparable properties in the area. Up to three-quarters of remortgages and up to a fifth of home purchases are now valued in this way. It is thought that the trend will continue towards an ever-increasing number of AVMs. An alternative is 'drive by' valuations, where qualified surveyors review properties from the available digital information, which is again a process that is on the increase.

Since everything is highly automated, much of the approvals process can all be completed in minutes, as opposed to the days or even weeks that it once took.

Alternatively, if as a potential buyer you haven't yet found your ideal home and were waiting to see how much you could spend, digitization of the process still plays an important role. It is possible to go through the process and get an automated approval in advance. This 'pre-approval' gives home buyers a high degree of confidence over how much they've got to spend, as well as something concrete to show estate agents. The pre-approvals are rock solid too, because they are based on exhaustive and completely accurate digital searches into a person's finances.

The improvements to the process certainly don't end once you find a mortgage and move in either. Thanks to the technology on offer, digital brokers aim to establish an ongoing relationship with you, so don't be surprised if they do all they can to establish a rapport. Rather than ignoring you until a few months or weeks before your fixed rate expires, as traditional mortgage companies often do, these digital broker apps will constantly review your mortgage to make sure you are on the right product. If a better, more appropriate, rate comes along, they'll get in touch and make a recommendation. They'll already have all the information they need about your financial circumstances, potential exit penalties and the best current rates.

Digital brokering is mainly handled in the virtual world. However, prospective home buyers are always given the option of talking to a human being if they so wish. There is no compulsion to do so though. What it all adds up to is a quick, convenient service. Right from the beginning, when you first think about buying a home, a digital mortgage application is a lot less stressful because it doesn't require so much effort.

Best for: established digital broker

To gain an insight into how much consumers are already embracing digital mortgage brokers, here's an interesting fact: in the United States, Quicken Loans, with its mortgage app *Rocket*, has overtaken Wells Fargo,[2] which has long held the distinction of being the largest originator of mortgage loans there. *Rocket*, which was launched in 2016, was one of the first mortgage lending offerings to give customers the ability to complete the entire loan process online. In minutes.

Rocket aims to make the process of getting a mortgage as intuitive and casual as possible. Well, as casual as it is possible to be when committing to what could be a six-figure loan. Would-be home buyers begin by entering basic information and choosing a goal such as 'lower your monthly payment'. Once you enter the details of the property address, *Rocket* uses publicly available data to pre-populate much of the form. The borrower's assets and credit history can be checked direct online with 98 per cent of US financial institutions, and income and employment information are downloaded in the same way.

If at any time the process isn't clear, applicants can click on question mark icons to answer specific questions or go through to a 'Talk to Us' section to speak to a real-life broker. It takes just minutes to get to a 'see solutions' page where *Rocket* reveals the choices of loans on offer. Pull-down menus allow applicants to customize the loan options such as changing the term or comparing fixed with variable rates. Once happy, there is the option to click on 'see if I am approved'. This is the stage where *Rocket* verifies all the information and submits the application to an automated underwriting system.

An application can be completed in around half an hour, although *Rocket* is keen to emphasize that the most important part is that buyers go at their own pace. Once at the underwriting stage, applicants move to a Facebook-style wall, where all the information is clearly laid out with to-do lists. This is the way the loan's progress is monitored right the way through until closing.

In the UK, *Atom* has a mortgage product that aims to digitize as much of the process as possible, with minimal manual intervention. At the time of writing, the mobile mortgage lender says it can provide an offer in three hours and has progressed an application to completion in nine working days.

Apps for that: *Rocket, Atom*

Best for: speedy applications and approvals

UK-based firms *Habito, Trussle, Mojo* and *MortgageGym* are all digital broker apps. As a customer, you pay nothing for digital services like these. The apps receive a fee from the lender when the borrower completes their home loan. The process begins with an online questionnaire that covers the basics of what you earn, the state of your finances, property type and the size of deposit available, all of which are used to complete a profile. Questionnaires take no more than 15 minutes, and once the details are acquired, automated engines take over, aggregating, verifying and analysing information to make a tailored mortgage recommendation.

Clearly lenders need to make sure they are happy to lend to you, which means they need to fully understand your financial situation. Thus, after you register with a digital broker app, it connects to your usual financial institutions and banks (with your permission, of course). *Habito* is part of *Starling*'s marketplace, for example, while *Rocket* and other US-based rivals such as *Roostify* and *Better Mortgages* retrieve their applicants' financial information directly from an applicant's bank. Once again, it's a great example of the increased connectivity brought about by open banking, which plays a crucial role in speeding up the process. Not only does this mean that mortgage applicants have to spend less time poring over piles of baffling paperwork, it also eliminates the need to send over copies of bank statements and proofs of identity numerous times. The data contained in customer records makes the process of verifying your assets and liabilities even easier too. Streamlining the process also means lower processing costs, improved accuracy and less risk of anything going awry that could slow things down later on. The beauty of everything being online is that the process can be broken up into digestible chunks, which makes everything straightforward and therefore much less stressful.

Apps for that: *Habito, Trussle, Mojo, MortgageGym, Roostify, Better Mortgage*

Crack conveyancing

Securing a mortgage agreement can be a nail-biting experience, but the place where the progress often breaks down is conveyancing.

Conveyancing is the legal process where an agreement is made to transfer a property from one person to another. It involves a highly complex series of steps, led by specialist property lawyers who handle all the legal paperwork, taking care of Land Registry and local council searches, drafting the contract and processing the exchange of money. Along the way lawyers undertake a painstaking search for anything you need to be aware of, such as any building control issues, nearby road schemes, or even potential environmental issues with contaminated land in the immediate surroundings. They also need to scrutinize property chains and make fraud and anti-money laundering checks. With potentially hundreds of pages of documents to process, it is a lengthy process and the long to-do list can, not surprisingly, slow everything down to a grinding halt. The sheer scale of the task means it can be expensive too, costing well in the region of a four-figure sum.

Now, if you were aiming for a truly digital mortgage, the entire transaction would be produced, transferred and stored electronically without using a single piece of paper. There would be no weighty loan file or agreement documents to sign with a 'wet' signature. In truth, we are not quite there yet, but there are definite signs we are well on the way. Certainly, many of the most important elements in the process are either within the sights of fintechs or are well under development.

Interestingly, some of these developments have been led by governments, which (a cynic might say) are never usually renowned for being at the cutting edge. However, it seems the authorities are keen to keep pace with leaps in technology. In the UK, HM Land Registry, which records all land and property ownership and mortgages in England and Wales, has made changes to the rules to pave the way for fully digital conveyancing documents with e-signatures. Since 6 April 2018, it has been possible to buy and sell homes without the need for paper deeds. The idea is to speed up the final stage of the process, and property sales can now be completed without the need for a witness to physically watch as the new homeowner manually signs a mortgage deed.

In the absence of the whole of the rest of the process being fully digitized in the immediate future, one area that is crying out for technological intervention is a system to ensure everyone always knows exactly what is going on. I'm choosing my words carefully here, but some solicitors do tend to work at their own pace. There are certainly opportunities to improve transparency around the information available (or not yet available), so anxious home buyers know exactly what is happening each step of the way. Greater visibility would ease at least some of the stress around the long-running lack of certainty over move dates, or last-minute changes.

Best for: digital case tracking

While digital case tracking is becoming more common online, it is not always as detailed as some would like. Would-be buyers are still frequently left in the frustrating position of not knowing whether a particular milestone has been reached, but at the same time worrying about hassling their legal representative with constant calls. Fortunately, there are some apps that make the process more transparent. With UK-based *When you move*, buyers and sellers can track each stage of their property transaction in real time, right through to completion. Everyone else involved in the process can use the mobile app to get live updates too, including estate agents, mortgage brokers and solicitors. Documents, letters and searches can be loaded onto the app, which can be accessed by all sides as required. Conveyancers are encouraged to publish updates at least every 72 hours, even if it is only to say, 'still waiting on the estate agent to send the sales memo'.

Alternatively, there is *eWay* from My Home Move, which is another UK offering that has also partnered with *Habito*. *eWay* is an online, case management tool that allows home buyers to manage their case 24/7 via their mobile or tablet. Again, documents can be uploaded onto the app and regular reminders are sent to keep things on track. The app has also partnered with a network of experienced conveyancers to integrate all the services under one roof.

US mortgage apps have been making similar strides, and *Rocket* has digitized the closing process in partnership with *Pavaso*, so home buyers can complete the process online.

Completing the process digitally, end-to-end, from the moment a prospective buyer thinks about moving, or spots their dream home, right up until the day they get the keys to the front door, is the aim for many providers. It is expected that many more fintechs will head this way.

Apps for that: *When you move*, *eWay*, *Pavaso*

Pre and post sales services

The scale and complexity of getting a mortgage means most people will continue to value some sort of human interaction. For now at least. All the apps mentioned in this chapter make much of the opportunity they offer to interact with real advisers who are on hand to address any pressing concerns. Over time, the emphasis on human interaction will almost certainly change. While three in five customers currently prefer to speak to an adviser about their mortgage (alongside their digital application), two in five customers already note that robo-advice will be faster and more convenient.[3]

As we begin to grow used to robo-advisers and see our friends and family benefiting from their help too, I predict the scope of this market will expand beyond the simple mortgage transaction. In fact, everything about the home buying journey is up for grabs. Instead of confining themselves to affordability calculations, digital brokers will inevitably begin to offer automated advice on the home as an investment and discuss where it sits within a consumer's broader financial profile. A home is, after all, a significant asset. Robo-advisers may well go on to suggest, or even pre-approve, complementary financial services products such as life insurance, either during or after the sales process. As you near completion, your digital adviser may helpfully advise on ATMs near your new house, or on competitively priced loans to fund the home improvements you may like to make. It could give a run down on the best current credit card rates to finance all the small purchases you may need when you move in. You'll already have a relationship with the adviser, who will have all the pertinent details, so why not?

Apps for that: Watch this space!

Notes

1　Experian [accessed 21 December 2017] How can technology play a part in mortgages [Online] www.experian.co.uk/blogs/latest-thinking/decisions-and-credit-risk/how-can-technology-play-a-part-in-digital-mortgages/

2　Forbes [accessed 5 February 2018] Quicken loans overtakes Wells Fargo as America's largest mortgage lender [Online] www.forbes.com/sites/samanthasharf/2018/02/05/quicken-loans-overtakes-wells-fargo-as-americas-largest-mortgage-lender/#17af160b264f

3　Accenture [accessed 9 June 2016] 2016 North America Consumer Digital Banking Survey [Online] www.accenture.com/t20160609T222453__w__/us-en/_acnmedia/PDF-22/Accenture-2016-North-America-Consumer-Digital-Banking-Survey.pdf

CHAPTER NINE

Give generously

It's easy to dismiss the digital generation as self-absorbed, selfie-snapping narcissists, but the reality is far from the truth. Technology hasn't made us more selfish, far from it. Better informed, yes, more connected, yes, but selfish? Not even close.

For a start, technology and, in particular, social media, has made us much more inclined to share. Most people share at least something online, whether it is their relationship status, or an inspiring video, or a big news update about something in their business or personal life. Whatever we share is linked directly to who we are.

One big beneficiary of this growing self-awareness has been charitable causes. When people care passionately about something, they frequently want to shout it from the rooftops, or at the very least get others to buy into their point of view. The opportunity to do this digitally has helped generate millions of pounds and dollars for charity. You may well remember viral events like the Ice Bucket Challenge that dominated social media through the summer of 2014. The idea, in aid of the charity ALS

Association, which supports research into a progressive neurodegenerative disease, raised US $115 million. Even the former US president George Bush accepted the challenge, along with dozens of well-known names from Mark Zuckerberg, to Bill Gates, to Oprah Winfrey, to Justin Bieber and Selena Gomez. In the same year, the idea of the 'no make-up selfie' caught on and helped increase the profile of Cancer Awareness. As well as ordinary folk 'daring to bare' and raising millions for charity, celebrities such as Kim Kardashian and J.Lo joined in. Meanwhile, Movember, which started life in Australia in the early 2000s, has grown to become a worldwide event for the Movember Foundation and has raised a fortune for men's health charities.

While these popular viral events spread like wild fire, that doesn't mean we are not choosy about the charities we support. Far from it, in fact. Thanks to the internet, we are generally better informed and, now we know so much more about everyone and everything, we've grown accustomed to scrutinizing things more closely and seeing them for what they really are. Gone are the days when a big organization or institution could raise money for a cause simply because, well, they were the biggest in the sector. Consumers tend to be far more critical and want to know a lot more about the causes they are giving to. There is an overwhelming desire to feel *inspired* by how our donations are being spent. We want to see and hear the story to make sure whatever we are buying into is authentic. Once again, a personal connection with the cause or the people that support it is crucial.

This philosophy also extends to the brands we support. If a big business wishes to claim a commitment to social values, they had better be fully committed. Authenticity is essential. If they can prove that they are genuine, the rewards are self-evident. In fact, 90 per cent of global consumers say they'd switch brands to one that is associated with a good cause, as long as the price and quality of the goods in question were equal to a rival brand that did not have quite such worthy intentions.[1]

Interestingly, a lot of disruptive new brands we're seeing centre around a more trusting, caring society. Think about Airbnb as a case in point. The marketplace for people to list and book lodgings has been built on the belief we trust each other enough to let other people stay in our homes. That's quite a big deal, isn't it? The new open banking opportunities, which have resulted in a proliferation of hugely useful new finance apps, rely on you, the customer, being happy to share your data with selected partners. In the chapter on insurance, I described how many of the new insurtech apps have based their business models on community spirit and trust between groups. This trend towards trust is all good news for the charitable sector.

However, while we are all becoming more sharing and caring, it doesn't naturally follow that money will effortlessly flood in to good causes. Not-for-profits need to tune into the *zeitgeist*, but they also need to make it easy to give in a digital world. Speed and convenience are key today: anyone who is inclined to donate is much more likely to do so if there is a quick and straight forward way to do so. This is why charities are focussing on making donating as simple as tapping for an Uber. Digital technology, with its access to innovative payment options, makes it easier for us to connect with the causes we believe in and make one-off or regular donations.

It is still early days in the digital disruption of charitable donations. According to Blackbaud's 2017 Charitable Giving Report, online donations represent only 7.6 per cent of charitable funding. However, that figure is growing fast and is up 12 per cent over the previous year. One of the most significant growth areas is donation via smart phones, which now account for 21 per cent of online giving. Since fewer and fewer people carry cash with them these days, these figures are expected to rise. Indeed, we've already seen a number of charities equip their street volunteers with contactless readers and chip and pin terminals. Early results show that supporters give *three* times as much when making a contactless payment.

In the following section, I have laid out some of the other innovative ways charities are making it easier for us to donate.

Microdonations: every penny counts

The cost of processing cheques and credit card payments has always made accepting small amounts in donations prohibitive for charities. One of the joys of digital is it immediately opens up the potential for organizations to accept donations of any size, however small. The donor also gets the satisfaction that the money they generously donate goes to the intended cause, rather than being swallowed up in excessive bank processing fees.

Welcome to the world of microdonations. The idea behind them is that making an impact isn't about the size of your wallet. If we all gave a £1 or US $1 to a good cause, and encouraged our friends to do the same, it would soon add up.

One of the earliest fintechs to see the potential of microdonations was UK-based *Pennies*. Dubbing itself the 'digital charity box', it works with retailers to enable microdonations to be made at the till. It's very similar to the traditional charity boxes you see on the counter, which are a great place to empty your small change into, but in this case it works via an option to add on a small amount to the bill. No data changes hands. There's simply a yes or no choice on the key pad, a payment device at the checkout prompting for a voluntary donation set between 1p and 99p. *Domino Pizza* was an early adopter, adding the donate button to its online orders back in November 2010. Today, over 50 different brands have deployed the service including *Evans Cycles*, *The Entertainer* and *Screwfix*.

The next logical step in digital microdonations has been to put technology right into our hands. Literally. There are now a growing number of apps that let you donate small amounts to causes you like, as and when you like.

Best for: regular giving

Spotfund, a US-based app, encourages donors to share their fundraising efforts for a range of causes via social media. Users simply drop a token onto a story to contribute US $1, $2 or $3 and then share via the app with the hope the cause may even go viral. It even gamifies the process, creating an 'impact score' showing the amount you've raised, plus the amount you've got friends to give too. It's possible to create a cause of your own to raise funds for something that matters to you. Another similar app is *Google One Today*, which enables users to donate US $1 a day and guarantees 100 per cent of the donation goes to the charity. It also offers a year-end tax receipt detailing all your charity transactions. *ShareTheMeal* collects microdonations for the World Food Programme.

Apps for that: *Spotfund, Google One Today, ShareTheMeal*

Best for: digital 'spare change'

Another microdonation approach is to collect our digital 'spare change' to put towards good causes. *Coin Up* was one of the first mobile donation apps approved for Apple's app store. When you make a purchase via your credit or debit card, the sum is rounded up and users of the app can direct the funds to an organization of their choice. All that is required is to sign up to the app, create an account and complete a three-step process that includes inputting your payment details to register to donate to a specific charity. Experiments are also under way with all sorts of contactless payment accessories, such as key rings and bracelets, which will help ease the process for donors to give spare change to charities every time they shop. The idea behind this is that donors buy a contactless accessory and load it with money linking it with a credit card. Each time the accessory is used to pay for a purchase, from a coffee to a railcard, it triggers a donation. Users will be able to manage the process and set donation limits as well as a cap to ensure they don't exceed a certain amount each month. Other spare change apps include *GiveTide*, *ChangeUp* and *RoundUp*.

Apps for that: *Coin Up*, *GiveTide*, *ChangeUp*, *RoundUp*

Best for: impulse donations

The fintech charity industry business is becoming ever more innovative too. *Snapdonate* is an app that enables you to donate small (and large) amounts on impulse. So, imagine you were boarding a train and spotted an advert for, say, Macmillan Cancer Support. Simply point your phone at the charity logo and take a picture via the *Snapdonate* app, choose how much you want to donate and you're done. You've given on the go. No SMS numbers to record or QR codes to fiddle with. It works anywhere too, whether you are out and about, on a train, or at home reading a magazine. *Snapdonate* automatically recognizes dozens of charity logos but can also send a donation to any of the 13,000 plus charities registered on JustGiving. The app deducts nothing for each gift, but JustGiving charges its usual 5 per cent handling fee.

App for that: *Snapdonate*

Best for: no cash giving

On the other side of the coin to microdonations are apps where you don't give a penny but *influence* where charitable donations are made. *Donate a Photo* and *Charity Miles* are two examples from the United States. *Donate a Photo* capitalizes on all those photos you take by turning them into cash for good causes. For every photo you share through *Donate a Photo*, US $1 is given to a good cause. The pictures become part of the *Donate a Photo* gallery but are not used for commercial purposes other than for the promotion of the app. With *Charity Miles*, all you need to do is download the app and, after that, every mile you walk, run or cycle sees money donated to your chosen charity, as long as you share your workout on social media. *Hold on*, you may be thinking. *There's no such thing as something for nothing.* Which is true. The money is coming from corporate sponsors. In the case of *Donate a Photo*, it's Johnson & Johnson, and *Charity Miles* has a panel of sponsors including Johnson & Johnson (again), Del Monte Fresh and Brooks Running. Organizations often give a proportion of their revenue to charity, and, thus, instead of giving the money directly, they choose to give it via an app. Your actions, in using the app, just influence where the money is spent (and get people sharing hashtags).

Apps for that: *Donate a Photo, Charity Miles*

Give more than money

Donating money is just one way to help worthy causes. If you are keen to do something worthy, there are a huge range of ways to get involved and, once again, digital is paving the way in helping us to gain a whole new perspective about helping others.

Best for: giving unwanted goods a new purpose

Gone for Good is an app that makes it even easier to declutter our homes and hand over unwanted items to charity. It aims to see an end to the days of lugging bags full of clothes and books to your nearest charity shop. This app has brought the process of donation bang up to date. Partnering with a range of causes, including The British Heart Foundation, Cancer Research UK, Mind, Oxfam, Shelter and the Salvation Army, *Gone for Good* simply requires you to upload photos of your unwanted items to the app. The app then liaises with the various charities that collect the belongings from your home.

It's great for larger items such as sofas, which you might otherwise pay to get taken away. It also ensures less clothing ends up in landfill. The people behind the app say that if they divert just 6 per cent of goods that would otherwise be thrown away, charity income will double. Users can also opt into Gift Aid, so the charity gets more cash at no extra cost to them.

App for that: *Gone for Good*

Best for: volunteering

If you wish to do more than donate cash and want to become even more involved, then volunteering is a great option. It's a hugely rewarding thing to do. Indeed, the founder of the US volunteering app *GiveGab* came up with the idea after reading a study that found that if we volunteer once a month, our happiness increases more than if our salary is doubled. Use the app to build a profile and then search for opportunities at charities that support interests close to your heart. The *GiveGab* app allows you to sign up online, or provides the organization's contact details. You can log your hours as you volunteer and even share photos and reflections, which appear on the app's social newsfeed 'The Gab'.

In the UK, there are several similar initiatives. *Team London* encourages people to sign up for a range of community activities from cleaning up to volunteering at events. There are specialist apps, such as *Be My Eyes*, that connects blind users with sighted volunteers who communicate via video link to provide any assistance needed. *GoodSam* is another great idea, which enables people to directly alert trained volunteer first aiders to attend the scene of medical emergencies. If you do volunteer, enjoy the experience and feel that you've done something worthwhile, then the *Ripil* app lets you log your stories and encourage others to do the same.

Apps for that: *GiveGab, Team London, Be My Eyes, GoodSam, Ripil*

Note

1   Cone Communications [accessed 27 May 2015] Ebiquity study: Global CSR [Online] www.conecomm.com/research-blog/2015-cone-communications-ebiquity-global-csr-study

CHAPTER TEN

Bill management made easy

The fundamental idea behind paying for stuff has not changed for centuries: the delightfully simple concept centres around the ability to transfer an agreed amount of money from one party to another. However, the way we make payments is changing at an almost dizzying pace today and is becoming even more simple and straightforward. In fact, the payment landscape has shifted more in the 2010s than it has over the last 25 years put together. We've come a very long way since the first encrypted online payment was made in 1994. (The transaction in question, if you are interested, was for the Sting album *Ten Summoner's Tales*.) Since then, we've seen a boom in online shopping, the rise of electronic bill payments, a growth in contactless and text payments and mobile wallets. There are now more than 350 different ways available to pay, and there are rapid moves to change this even further in the future.

Digital bill management

Missing a bill payment once in a while might seem pretty insignificant (we all make mistakes, right?), but do it too often and it can play havoc with your credit score. Once that goes awry, it can take a lot of work to recover your previous good standing (for advice on this, see Chapter 4 'Check your credit score'). It is, of course, possible to set a bill reminder on your calendar and then respond as and when, but in reality, a reminder isn't always enough motivation to actually pay on the day. What's more, when you have to dig out the bill itself and organize a debit, the impetus to do it can fade even further.

Bill payment apps are a neat way of scheduling bills to be paid to the various providers you use, all from the same source, ensuring bills are always paid correctly and in good time. The service is often free, although that sometimes depends upon whether you use a bank account or credit card to make the payments.

There are different plus points for many of the bill payment apps that are currently available.

Best for: simple reminders

At the simplest end of things is *BillTracker*, which is basically a calendar-based reminder service of when a water bill, car payment or mobile subscription is due. There's also a quick view function that shows a breakdown of all upcoming bills, along with the amount owed, so users can keep tabs on what's coming up next.

App for that: *BillTracker*

Best for: active management of bills

Bean connects to your bank account and credit cards to track all of your regular bill payments and subscriptions to services like Netflix, Spotify and Apple Music. Payments are broken down and presented on a clear dashboard, so you can see what is going out and when. What is interesting about this app is that as well as quickly showing up any unwanted subscriptions you may have simply forgotten to cancel, *Bean* will also go on to unsubscribe for you if you so wish. Traditionally, it is up to you to contact each individual organization that you have signed up with, which is why we are often too lazy to act. The app reckons we waste up to £223 a year on unwanted subs, so that could mean quite a saving. This app will also highlight the availability of better deals elsewhere with the utilities you use, or whether you might be missing out on a keener rate on your credit card. *Bean* is a service that estimates it could save households a further £672 a year. Users can sign up for smart notifications of potential savings, as well as tips on managing finances.

US bill management app *Hiatus* has many similar elements to *Bean* in that it focuses on all those free trials we sign up for and keeps track of subscriptions. Add in your monthly subscriptions, including the free trials you've signed up for, and it will remind you whenever a service is about to auto charge your account. If you are signed up for something you no longer want, or realize you've been 'accidently' paying for, it'll help you to cancel it directly from the app. It also monitors rates on outgoings such as mortgages and insurance, to make sure users stay on the best deal.

Apps for that: *Bean, Hiatus*

Best for: bill management, plus

Mint, the personal finance app, and *Onedox* both feature bill tracking and payment features alongside wider budgeting and credit check services. Like most bill management services, it allows you to streamline the whole process by organizing everything into one central location and then review, manage and pay when bills are due. Since this is just one of many features concerning your finances on the *Mint* app, it is possible to see how your spending relates to all your other financial obligations and goals.

Prism follows a similar pattern, minus the spending analytics, but it is also possible to pay bills directly through the free app, instead of via a third-party processor. Simply link the payment accounts that you use to pay your bills and away you go. When a new bill is available, *Prism* sends a push notification to your phone letting you know you need to schedule a payment. App users have the choice of paying the bill immediately or scheduling it to be paid sometime in the future. And, since third-party payments are not involved, any overlooked bills can be paid instantly.

Prism, like many bill management apps, incorporates a feature to notify a user if a bill looks out of the ordinary compared with previous usage. It's a really useful device that prompts you to double check the bill and, if necessary, put things right.

Apps for that: *Mint, Onedox, Prism*

Best for: accurate record keeping

If you've ever scrabbled around trying to find old copies of utilities bills, you'll appreciate *Doxo*, which also works like a digital filing cabinet, as well as a bill payment hub. US-based *Doxo* automatically collects electronic statements from various providers, from utility companies to banks, and saves them all in one central account. It is also possible to upload other family and household documents and save them in your online filing cabinet.

App for that: *Doxo*

Energy and utilities

Energy companies and banks share a very similar legacy. They are both centralized, heavily regulated structures that are built on complex processes. Interestingly, the energy business is currently in the process of a disruptive shake-up just like banking, although it is still quite early days in this respect.

There is a widespread view that it is high time technology were introduced to completely transform the idea of paying for services such as energy and utilities. One of the most interesting ideas to come out so far is to change the traditional model entirely. Instead of you, the consumer, paying one of a handful of utility giants in currency, via direct debit, or even bitcoin, what if you didn't pay a mega utility firm at all? What if, for example, you could buy and sell energy among your friends and neighbours? You could become your own energy supplier.

Peer-to-peer energy trading, which cuts out the middleman entirely, is just one of the many business models currently being explored. The power (excuse the pun) is being put into the hands of the consumers of energy, who are becoming energy *producers* too. The catchy new name for this category is prosumers. Prosumers are not restricted to buying from a single large-scale supplier who acts as a middleman, selling energy and utility services to individual households. Instead, prosumers can simply trade electricity with each other and receive payments on the spot, in real time, from an entirely automated system. All they need is a solar panel on their roof and the technology in place to buy and sell energy.

Best for: energy switching

If you are not quite ready to become an energy supplier the very least you should be doing is making sure you get the best possible deal for all your energy needs. We all owe it to ourselves to check our bills and stay on top of the prices we are paying. Forget to check and you could end up hundreds of pounds a year out of pocket. Handily, there are a whole bunch of energy switching firms, which take all the pain out of checking suppliers and then, if necessary, moving to a new one. Auto switching energy apps such as *lookaftermybills*, *Labrador* and *Switchcraft*, work a little like price comparison sites, but instead of just listing the best deals, they monitor the market and, if there is a better tariff, they automatically move you across and take care of the whole switch. The services are all free, with the apps receiving their income via commission from energy suppliers. Customers get to set preferences, such as if they prefer renewable energy suppliers.

Apps for that: *lookaftermybills*, *Labrador*, *Switchcraft*

Best for: sharing solar

US-based *LO3 Energy* has developed a system that lets people who have installed solar panels on their roof or on their land sell any excess energy to people nearby via so-called smart grids. To get started, users install smart meters to track the energy their solar panels generate versus the amount their household consumes. An electronic ledger underpins the transactions, carefully logging the excess and managing the sale of the excess to nearby neighbours. As well as being efficient, it has the added green bonus that distributing energy this way is more efficient and environmentally friendly than transmitting it over large distances. So far, this system has been working successfully in Brooklyn, New York, and is now being rolled out elsewhere. There are two similar projects in Germany where millions of homes benefit from solar panels fitted to their roofs. However, here consumers are obliged to sell any excess power back to the grid at a price set by the major utility firms.

App for that: *LO3 Energy*

Best for: energy trading

In the UK, *Electron* is developing what has been dubbed an 'energy eBay', where utilities can work together to balance supply and demand. Under the plan, consumers will be compensated for adjusting their energy consumption to use a greater amount in periods where there is a good supply of renewable energy, and less when there is a relatively low supply. Thus consumers can run appliances such as washing machines and dishwashers 'off peak' to qualify for lower tariffs. The process relies on blockchain technology, which allows direct transactions between all parties and links the whole process to smart-home technology. At the time of writing, it has yet to be launched, but it does have backing from some big names in energy such as Siemens and National Grid.

Best for: electric car owners

In Germany *Share&Charge* is an app that connects electric cars with available charging stations, both residential and commercial. Drivers of electric cars can relax in the knowledge they'll easily be able to find a charging point while out on the road. Vehicle owners can also register their own charging points and determine their own rate for the service.

The underlying technology coordinates the charging station network and the system shows drivers where nearby stations are located on an interactive map that also shows how they are being used.

App for that: *Share&Charge*

CHAPTER ELEVEN

Saving for retirement

The low stress way

While all sorts of digital innovations that transform the way we interact with our cash are bursting onto the scene at a fantastic rate, one of the sectors that has thus far lagged behind in the money revolution is pensions. Indeed, even today, most pension savers will attest to the fact that they are still scrambling around trying to manage accounts via paper-based information located in various files. With some of the documentation stretching back for years, this is no easy task even for the most organized of households.

There are a number of reasons behind the lack of urgency in modernizing pension provision. For a start, there has simply not been such a widespread demand for action as there has been for a better version of other existing financial products, such as budgeting and banking. For many, particularly the younger, more digitally savvy generation, the need for a pension seems, well, just so far off. There are legacy issues fuelling this apparent lethargy too. Most people in previous generations could rely on a final salary scheme where the outcome was predetermined. There simply wasn't a need to engage with pensions until even the last few months before retirement. Everyone could be pretty confident of exactly where they were and what they were due. Even today, now that most final salary schemes have long since gone the way of the dinosaur, that view that 'everything is sorted' hasn't really disappeared. Typically, it is not until people reach 50, or older, that the 'r' word looms. There has been no rush to change the status quo.

It doesn't help that pensions have always been notoriously difficult to unravel. In fact, working out what we will have and when we'll have it can involve a long, slow and laborious process. Someone, somewhere has had to compile all our scheme details (after we've hunted out all those elusive pieces of paper), and make sure there are no policies we've forgotten about. In the UK, pension laws have been softened since April 2015, with the aim of making the process a little easier and affording the over 55s full freedom to spend their retirement savings how they wish. Previously, retirees found themselves being shoehorned into annuity schemes, which meant inviting insurers to provide proposals, comparing options, assessing the impact of various variables and so on. Today, anyone aged 55 and over with a private pension can take a quarter of their pension as a tax-free lump sum, and then draw down on the rest through retirement. This means more choice, which is great, but the risks of getting it wrong and miscalculating are high, so this only adds to the atmosphere of tension around the whole business of pensions.

All that paper shuffling and general confusion is about to change. A lot of what will come next is down to APIs, which are a really good thing for your pension pot.

I've mentioned APIs, or in full, Application Programming Interfaces, already a few times in *The Money Revolution*, but it might be helpful to give a bit more background here. APIs are sets of standards that allow software components to talk to one another and allow interactions between different systems to happen. By publishing APIs for a system, you enable developers the world over to build your system's capabilities into their own software. APIs enable emails and texts to be sent easily from any app, restaurant or hotel searches to reach into the databases of myriad chains and Google maps to enrich any apps' user interface. This sort of frictionless communication between various businesses is the technology that allows you to, say, effortlessly book a stay at a Marriott in Sri Lanka via *Booking.com*. Published APIs make app developers' lives a lot easier because if they want to build a whizz bang app, they don't need to start from scratch every time. They simply integrate all the APIs they need in order to achieve the product they want and to make it do the things they want it to do. The availability of more abundant and sophisticated APIs is one of the reasons behind the proliferation and variety of financial technology products in recent years. This process of sharing, which is as beneficial to you and me as it is to developers, is also another tick in the box for the open banking initiative. With everyone sharing APIs, we all benefit.

The reason for diverting to this short bit of techie speak is to explain how it is APIs (and the sharing of them) that we have to thank for the fact pensions are finally being cracked open. They are at the centre of advances to manage the risk of something going wrong when we tackle these crucial, long-term savings plans.

APIs make everything to do with pensions so much easier, linking all the parties involved, connecting up all the various policies and bridging the gap between all the numerous systems and options. Apply APIs to pensions and suddenly everything becomes a lot clearer and simpler to manage. With apps enabled with APIs to all the pensions providers, you may no longer need to spend hours rummaging through paperwork to put together a full picture of your retirement planning.

It's not just about sorting out what you've got and where it is, before putting it all together to better manage it in one location. The use of this technology allows firms to share specific details and consumer data with a wider audience of potential insurers, which means pricing options come in faster and, with more competition, they should be keener too. Similarly, since the policies are so easy to view and collate, it is also easier to track them effectively over time and make adjustments as necessary. One of the potential upsides of long-term investments like pensions is most people have time to adjust and change course, in order to secure the best possible outcome. These advances make that process much, much easier.

It's all happening in the nick of time too. In recent years we have seen the mass auto enrolment of savers into new workplace pensions. These new schemes rely on individuals making important decisions about where they want their money invested. New developments in pension technology will allow for an increased engagement with our retirement funds to ensure we have the best possible retirement pot.

Visibility and consolidation of pension pots

At the very simplest level, the new generation of pension apps will show you an instant snapshot of your pension savings via online dashboards. Instead of waiting for an annual review, or worse still, staying in blissful ignorance until just a few months before retirement, it is possible to use your mobile phone to check your balances anytime, anywhere. One of the useful features of apps like these are the facility to model how much you need to invest, based on your current age and salary, in order to get the retirement you desire. In the UK, the government is expected to launch its own pensions dashboard in 2019, which will allow people to access their information from most places online. However, the service is mooted to be quite basic and will not allow for any sort of consolidation of the various pension pots.

Obviously, there are risks involved if you decide to transfer your pension between existing schemes. If there is an exit fee from your current policy, the app you choose will let you know. If existing policies with guarantees are transferred, such as those with a guaranteed annuity rate, or a final salary promise, you will be sent the relevant paperwork ahead of the transfer, so you can fully consider all options. If one of your existing pensions has guaranteed benefits that exceed £30,000, you are required to seek advice from a transfer specialist/financial adviser before you go ahead. This will all be highlighted in the apps.

Best for: simplicity

There are plenty of free tools available to help you take the first steps in planning for retirement by working out your current situation, which is a good start. Being more aware of what you have today is the starting point of taking control. It also paves the way to taking an active role in managing your pension pot, which will be streets ahead of a situation where you really had no clue, often until it was too late. Apps that help here include *Retirement Countdown* and *Retire Logix*. The basic idea is to see your savings to date and how much you will need to dedicate to saving in order to secure a comfortable retirement.

Apps for that: *Retirement Countdown, Retire Logix*

Best for: consolidation

With most adults changing jobs every few years, they often end up with having several small pension pots in various employer's schemes. Not only is it difficult to keep track of, but it is also easy to miss the fact that some of the money will be languishing in poorly performing funds with the double whammy of high charges eating away at the lump sum. *PensionBee* helps you track down all of your different pension pots via the names of your past and present employers. The app then consolidates all of the savings plans into one low-cost plan. You will be able to see the size of your current pension plan and your projected retirement income. You can then also set up regular further contributions with a few clicks. With a digital pension that is easily accessed from a phone, you will be constantly aware of any potential shortfall, and regular prompts to take action can only have a positive outcome.

It's worth pointing out that *PensionBee* has four plans to choose from, but does not provide specific recommendations or advice. As noted above, this is an issue for anyone with a final salary pension, or a fund that holds over £30,000 of guaranteed benefits, which means advice must be sought. Charges vary from 0.25 per cent to 0.95 per cent depending upon the plan and how much is invested.

App for that: *PensionBee*

Pension planning

There is no such thing as a job for life anymore, and no household can claim to be in prime financial health if the people within it have not made proper provision for life after work. According to the World Economic Forum (WEF), there is a US $70 trillion gap in the world's pension systems. (The gap is the amount of money required to provide each person with a retirement income equivalent to 70 per cent of their pre-retirement salary.) The United States accounts for US $28 trillion of that gap. Meanwhile, research by the Organisation of Economic Co-operation and Development (OECD)[1] shows the UK to have the least generous state pension of all advanced economies. Under current estimates, more than 10 million people face poverty in retirement. All of these figures are expected to climb markedly by 2050, when millennials begin to look seriously at taking a pension.

Whatever else you do by way of savings and investment, pension planning should be a priority. If you want to maintain your standard of living in retirement, private pensions are crucial to fill the gap. On average, you will need two-thirds of your final salary to live comfortably in retirement.

The good news is, pensions are among the most tax-efficient savings products available. In the UK, for example, residents under the age of 75 can make contributions of up to 100 per cent of their annual earnings before tax, subject to their available allowance, and receive 20 per cent tax relief.

While employers and employees are obliged to contribute a percentage of the employee's salary to a pension throughout his or her career (auto enrolment was introduced in the UK in 2012), and workplace pensions are an increasingly effective part of retirement planning, they are not everything. The minimal contributions are, well, minimal. To continue with the UK example, as of April 2019, there is an obligatory 3 per cent contribution for the employer with a further 5 per cent coming from the employee. While it is certainly well worth it, since paying into a pension gives all employees a tax break, it would be unwise for anyone to think that they've taken care of things on this level of investment. Don't let participating in a workplace pension scheme lull you into a false sense of security. Saving a single digit percentage of your earnings into your pension pot each year is highly unlikely to give you the comfortable retirement you desire.

Once again, it can seem like a tough call unravelling the best thing to do when it comes to topping up your pension, and this is why the new generation of pension apps are really handy, offering a service tailored to your specific circumstances. As with all pension advice, it is something you will need to pay for, but generally, digital managers cost a lot less than traditional advisers. An initial review with an IFA can cost as much as £500, with those looking for pension advice at retirement facing a potential charge of £1,000 on a fund of £100,000.

Digital charges are generally via an annual fee calculated as a percentage of your total pension, with the figure depending upon the size of your pot and how much of a tailored service you opt for. This generally includes fees to managers who look after your long-term investment. The scale of fees makes these online services quite competitive. The obvious question to ask is, are they safe? After all, the digital service will be dealing with potentially large sums and the money makes up our all-important life savings too. Like any of the apps mentioned in this book, they are fine in terms of data protection, because they use high level encryption to protect all your details. Plus, if the companies behind the apps were to go out of business, your capital would be protected under the Financial Services Compensation Scheme. However, as with all investments, there is always a risk you could lose some, or even all, of your money if the funds performed poorly.

Best for: flexibility

Nutmeg is one of the first digital services to take advantage of robo-advisers. It started life by initially offering ISAs and general investment accounts and moved into pensions in 2015. To set up a pension, users need to input their gender, age and when they plan to retire. *Nutmeg*'s pension calculator allows you to enter the desired retirement income and records of any current savings to calculate how much you'd need to save each month to make that target a reality by the desired age. Pension planners are then able to select from 10 different risk profiles, from least risky, 1, to most risky, 10. The calculator allows you to play around with risk levels to see how likely it is you'll reach your target based on opting for each particular level. *Nutmeg* will then take you through a risk assessment to build a profile based on your investing experience, understanding of risk and loss, and views on the stock market. The responses will lead to a recommendation of 1 out of 10 portfolios. Once the pension is up and running, users can alter contributions and risk levels at any point.

The minimum initial investment is £5,000, which is higher than many other services. Charges are 0.75 per cent up to £100,000 and 0.35 per cent beyond that.

Another similar app worth looking at is *Moneyfarm*, which is another in the new breed of robo-advisers for pensions. This service offers six risk levels and requires a minimum initial investment of £500. Investors then pay 0.7 per cent on the first £20,000, then 0.6 per cent on any amount from £20,000 to £100,000, and then 0.5 per cent from £100,000 to £500,000.

Apps for that: *Nutmeg, Moneyfarm*

Future developments in retirement cash flow

The biggest issue facing anyone in retirement is how long their money will last. Since the introduction of pension freedoms many people face the prospect their money might run out before they die. Add into the mix that lives are now more complex with divorces among the over 60s on the rise and debt becoming more prevalent, and it all becomes quite challenging.

In the past, thanks to final salary schemes, we all knew how much cash we'd be getting each month *throughout* our retirement. Former employers would faithfully continue to pay up as long as they needed to and retirement was as carefree as it is meant to be. Most workers today though are in defined contribution schemes, which means when we hit retirement age we have to hope for the best that the pot of money we have lasts. There is, of course, still the option of buying an annuity, which would pay out a fixed sum each year. That does have its downsides though and the sums on offer can be low. The best buy annuity deals today are around 5 per cent, so if you put in £100,000 you'd receive an income of just £5,000 per year. This would continue indefinitely though, until the pensioner died.

The alternative is a do-it-yourself version. Say, for example, that instead of an annuity you decided to take 7 per cent a year out of that same £100,000 pension pot. In other words, you drew £7,000 annually. Within 14 years, that pot would be empty.

Reduce your expectations to just 6 per cent and it would still only last just over 16 years.

It's worth pointing out at this stage that, on average, retirement lasts for 18.5 years for a man who takes his pension at 65 and 20.5 years for a woman. Based on the calculations here, there is a high probability indeed of some lean years ahead on a meagre state pension.

With the do-it-yourself approach, it is possible to take a lower income at first and invest capital in equity income funds. This will produce an income that, all being well, rises over time. More importantly, there is less chance of the funds running out. Alternatively, and preferably, you could plan well ahead of the event and use digital technology to forecast the projected size of your pension pot and what it would mean to your annual income year by year in retirement. How much can you take out each year without the risk of falling short?

Whatever way you look at it, attempting to manage this by yourself is challenging and extremely difficult. You'd need to factor in investment returns, liabilities and tax, to name but a few factors where any change could send your calculations spiralling off course. At the time of writing, there are still relatively few mobile apps offering to make this all easier, however it is within the sights of many of the larger pension providers such as *Arriva*, *Scottish Widows* and *Aegon*, as well as in the crosshairs of digital start-ups. Organizations are investing heavily in their digital pension strategies, and I confidently expect some innovative new ideas to emerge over the following few years.

Once again, watch this space.

Note

1 OECD [accessed 5 December 2017] Pensions at a glance 2017 [Online] www.oecd.org/unitedkingdom/PAG2017-GBR.pdf

CHAPTER TWELVE

Invest like a pro

Asset management describes the way that spare cash can be diverted to investments that pay a higher rate of return than traditional savings accounts, whether it be stocks and shares, property, commodities or international investments. Traditionally, this sort of thing has been the preserve of high net worth individuals. That is, until now. Hardly surprisingly, asset management is another sector of personal finance to come under the scrutiny of disruptors. There are, after all, clear opportunities to open it up to a wider community of investors. And it is high time too. Research shows that 80 per cent of the population don't save regularly.[1]According to The Money Charity, 9.6 million UK households have no savings whatsoever to count on.

It doesn't help that many people find talking or thinking about saving and investing boring. (According to Mintel, a third of British consumers either have 'low' or 'extremely low' interest in any sort of financial management.) I suspect many of those who say they are not interested (and, indeed, many who are) find it all a bit baffling and intimidating too. If you are not a City hotshot, how do you know you're investing in the right thing? Aren't you in danger of losing everything even if you take the minimum amount of risk?

The solution is, of course, to make it easy for people to invest small amounts of money on a regular basis and to cut out all the hours of research and paperwork that might usually go with picking strong investments. Thanks to the new generation of automated portfolio management, with its extremely low barriers of entry, this is now a reality. Investors can set their options and then let robots do the rest. If you want to invest (even a small amount), go right ahead. It makes little to no difference if apps are handling thousands of small transactions, rather than a few big ones. Moving money from one account to another is ridiculously simple. The digital culture also neatly overcomes traditional obstacles to investment, such as minimum entry requirements.

To judge just how effective this sort of digital strategy can be for investments both big and small, all you need to know is that some of the major City firms are taking it very seriously indeed. Money management giants like Goldman Sachs and New York hedge fund Two Sigma now use AI and machine learning for their trading strategies. It has been predicted that over the next 25 years, 99 per cent of investment management will be done in this way. And why not? Computers have repeatedly proved themselves adept at spotting investment opportunities that humans have missed. Machines can sift through vast quantities of data looking for significant patterns. They can dig far deeper into the data, generate hypotheses and test them, and all at a rate that far exceeds what can be achieved by mortal man or woman.

Ask the robo-adviser

For years, there has only been one of two options when it comes to making long-term investments. You could do it yourself, or you could employ an IFA to help you. The former is the low-cost, yet high workload option, and there is no guarantee that you'd get it right. With little or no experience, it is very easy to jump in or out of the market at entirely the worst time, which could lead to you losing everything.

The latter option, an IFA, presents an entirely different set of issues. For a kick off, it is not that long since IFAs promoted themselves on the basis that they gave 'free' advice. In reality, the advice was anything but free. Advisers made money through commission paid to them via fund managers. Thus, investors might end up paying up to 1 per cent or 2 per cent annually (or possibly even more) to their IFA. The downside here was the fees meant whichever investment vehicle you did decide to put your money into had to do 1 per cent or 2 per cent better than the market just to keep up. And, while it would be nice to believe the IFA always had your best interests at heart, history has proven this to not always be the case. A succession of scandals has shown that the temptation to line their own wallets led some IFAs to deliver advice that was not exactly measured or appropriate. The city watchdog, the Financial Conduct Authority (under its previous guise as the Financial Services Authority) called time on 'free advice' in 2012 and improved professional standards in the industry. However, an unexpected downside of this move was that it caused many advisers to exit the IFA business altogether, causing a shortage of qualified IFAs. And, as we all know, when there is a shortage, the fees go up for the services of the ones that remain. Independent advice is now mainly only available to those who are able to invest large amounts or who have a sizeable net worth. Basically, it has put investing out of the reach of many ordinary people.

But this is the case no more, thanks to robo-investors. Robo-investors are certainly not second best either. In fact, as well as offering a more accessible, cheaper service than human investors, robo-investors do a pretty effective job.

Robo-investors use software to automatically buy and sell assets, rebalancing a portfolio over time. They are not 'active investors', by which I mean they don't attempt to beat the market with their brilliant and insightful investing picks. Their model is passive, which means they buy and then hold a broadly diverse portfolio of assets without really messing with the mix. Rather than beating the market, the funds simply match whole market gains over time.

It is relatively easy to get started, certainly a lot quicker and simpler than working with a traditional IFA, who would expect a lengthy initial face-to-face interview, grilling the client on every aspect of their financial affairs and their attitude to risk before they came up with an investment strategy. With a robo-investor, there is typically an online questionnaire that can be carried out at any time, day or night, so is convenient to everyone. The result of the survey takes care of risk profiling. The data is fed into an algorithm that works out a suitable investment portfolio and then makes its recommendations. Customers are free to adjust the recommendation as they wish.

Robo-investors are not for everyone building an investment portfolio. If, for example, you have a large sum to invest of, say, over £100,000, you may well benefit from a more human touch. Why? Well, robo-advisers, so far, are great at buying and selling assets, but their recommendations are purely based on the information you provide during the online survey. While taking into account how much you have to invest, among a few other things, the automated service won't consider the interplay between your investment strategy and any other wealth you may have that is tied up in your home or pension, or any debts you might have. In short, robo-advisers can only ever work off the information you provide them with, according to the questions being asked, whereas an IFA would always look at the bigger picture. They ask follow-up questions based on their one-to-one interactions with clients. It is for this reason that human advisers still have a role to play in more complex situations such as planning for big events in the future like starting a business, buying a house, or managing a big lifestyle change.

However, if you are just starting out, or only have small sums to invest, robo-advisers could present the perfect introduction into this market. There are certainly definite advantages to them when it comes to clearly setting goals (how much you have to invest and how often) and in asset allocation (where you invest your cash).

Best for: entry-level robo-investment

Robo-investors such as *Nutmeg, Moneyfarm, evestor, Moola, Scalable Capital, WealthSimple* and *Wealthify* all have relatively low entry costs. Typically, annual fees range from 0.45 per cent of the value of the asset being advised upon, and this covers advice, portfolio management and administration. *Wealthsimple* has no minimum investment amount, while *Moneyfarm, evestor* and *Wealthify* have a minimum investment of just £1, which makes these apps especially accessible even to novice investors. However, some have a higher minimum investment threshold (*Nutmeg* requires £500, *Moola* £100 and *Scalable Capital* £10,000). Money can be invested as a lump sum or in instalments.

Investors are given an online questionnaire asking about their financial situation, investment experience and attitude to risk, before being given a personal recommendation on which investment portfolio would best suit their needs (the number of portfolios managed by each app varies among the apps). Investors can keep tabs on their portfolios via apps, but the human touch is still on offer through live webchats or the opportunity to arrange discussions via Skype.

It is important to keep an eye on the fees being charged, because even small fees can eat into your investment if they are being paid out year after year. Also, the old maxim that the value of your investment can go down as well as up applies here too.

Apps for that: *Nutmeg, Moneyfarm, evestor, Moola, Scalable Capital, WealthSimple, Wealthify*

Spare any change?

As you will have no doubt worked out by now, fintech is all about finding ways to demystify money and offer, simpler, low-cost ways to save and invest. Investing in the markets, or even in ISAs, may have seemed like a step too far for many in the past. Many people fear it will take just too much cash to get started, or may simply find the whole concept intimidating and confusing. Without the support of a qualified adviser, it is almost impossible to make smart decisions, right?

Again, app technology is working towards transforming this thinking. Your digital CFO is your friend who can make investing easy and, dare I say it, even enjoyable. And, the best part about it? Micro investing is fully automated, allowing you to reap the benefits for barely any work.

Micro investing is basically the act of saving very small amounts of money on a regular basis, and it is the pain-free answer to growing your savings. The basis of the idea is that apps can suck virtual spare change from our pockets and funnel it directly into an investment portfolio. The great thing about it is, the amounts are so small you barely notice that it has happened.

Over time, investing frequent small sums adds up. Sweep 20p a day to one side and it builds to £6 a month, or £72 a year. This might not sound like very much, but it is a start. Plus, it gets you into the habit of saving and that is never a bad thing.

While many investment platforms still have minimum starting limits of £500 or more, I suspect many more will be reducing their entry levels to as little as £1 in the coming months and years. 'Fractional trading', as it is known in the industry, where investors buy into funds selling fractions of whole shares, makes sense because it is pretty accessible to anyone and will introduce more customers into the market. I should, however, add one word of warning, over and above the usual 'the value of your investment can go down as well as up'. You also need to be realistic about the true value of what you are investing. It is easy to con yourself into thinking you're doing something significant, when you are actually only putting away a few pounds each month. At the other end of the scale, if you start to invest a lot more, you will end up paying higher fees.

There are now a handful of spare change investment apps that allow you to invest in stocks for very little outlay.

Best for: first time savers

MoneyBox was established to introduce younger generations to the idea of investing. The app is linked to a user's current account or credit card, and they can then select if they want to invest in a stocks and shares ISA or a Lifetime ISA. Risk appetite can be set to cautious, balanced or adventurous. Next, users select how much money they want to invest each week, and there is the facility to automatically round up everyday purchases made through a bankcard of their choice. Thus, if you bought a cappuccino for £2.70, you could round this up to £3 and invest the difference in a stocks and shares ISA. There's also a £10 'Quick add' button if you are feeling flush.

Another app, *True Potential*, gives savers the chance to put as little as £1 into a multi-asset fund. The average sum invested on the app is £10 and 75 per cent of the money invested in the app is under £50. For a tiny cost of entry, your cash is invested in funds managed by the likes of Goldman Sachs, Schroders, Allianz and 7IM.

What's remarkable about services like these is they give investors a whole new freedom. Where previously you would need to invest *at least* the cost of one whole share in a single company, which would cost a specific monetary amount like £56.98 per unit, you can now put in a fixed amount as low as a pound. It makes everything less tricky. Want to invest £10? Fine, go ahead. It is perfectly doable. And easy too.

It is worth noting that there are fees involved. With *MoneyBox*, for example, there is a £1 a month fee, a 0.45 per cent platform fee and fund fees ranging from 0.22 per cent to 0.24 per cent. This can add up to be quite significant on a small investment, but it needs to be weighed up against the fact it is a quick and easy way to get into the investment habit.

Apps for that: *MoneyBox*, *True Potential*

Note

1 BlackRock [accessed 17 June 2016] Spending in retirement ... or not [Online] www.blackrock.com/us/financial-professionals/your-practice/defined-contribution/news-insight-analysis

CHAPTER THIRTEEN

Travel cash best deals

Foreign travel is a great opportunity to challenge yourself, experience something a bit different and even gain some new skills and knowledge along the way. There may be a new language to get to grips with, an entirely unfamiliar cuisine to enliven your taste buds and a wonderful new culture to discover.

Interestingly though, when it comes to the money side of this experience, the majority of travellers prefer to stick with something rather familiar: that is cold, hard cash. While many people have long since embraced cash-free payments with everything from contactless to Apple Pay, somehow this all seems a step too far once we start making plans to hit foreign soil. In fact, 75 per cent of travellers[1] focus their trip-planning energies on arranging to withdraw cash for their trip, either beforehand or on arrival at their destination. One of the most favoured ways to load up on notes is to withdraw from ATMs on landing at the airport. In fact, 31 per cent of UK travellers withdraw their holiday cash immediately upon reaching their destination. Others don't even get that far, panicking at their domestic airport and withdrawing large amounts at in-terminal foreign exchange bureaux, where you pay a premium for the last-minute service through fairly uninspiring exchange rates.

Getting access to your money via foreign ATMs is a hugely expensive way of going about it too. In fact, it is estimated that UK travellers notch up £125 million in bank charges and foreign transaction fees each year by managing their travel spend in that way. Just one withdrawal can prompt a range of deductions. Your bank may charge up to 3 per cent in non-sterling transaction fees and there may also be a 2 per cent fee for using an overseas ATM. That's not the only thing that might leave you feeling a little out of pocket. Chances are, you'll lose out to something called Dynamic Currency Conversion (DCC). DCC is the exchange rate offered by the ATM machine. Rest assured, it is always, always a horrible rate. It is estimated that this can add up to 6 per cent to the cost of a transaction.

As if all this is not bad enough, there is another way your dream holiday can turn into a bit of a nightmare, cash-wise. As anyone who has ever used a foreign ATM will know, the card machine will often 'helpfully' ask if you would like to 'fix the exchange rate', or will mention that 'this ATM offers conversion to your home currency'. Occasionally, it doesn't even ask the question properly, or certainly the offer is couched in very vague terms that encourage the withdrawer towards the more expensive option. It may display, for example, the exchange rate, a sum of money in your own currency and a simple 'yes' or 'no' choice. Never, ever accept the offer to convert to your own currency: it will leave you much worse off. Always select no, or whatever option is offered that won't convert the sum into your own domestic currency. It's also worth noting that the same scenario frequently pops up on card terminals when you spend money in shops and restaurants. Again, *always* ask to pay in the local currency.

If you are not careful, that relaxing £2.50 coffee you tapped your card for as you idly relaxed in a piazza watching the world go by, could easily be inflated to £3.50. Maybe you'll be relaxed enough to chill out about the extra £1, but these sums do add up over a two-week holiday. Chances are, you'll have better uses for your cash than bank charges too.

Whatever way you look at it, holiday cash is a bit of a mine-field. Yet, there are a few very basic things that can be done to reduce liabilities. For a start, travellers should do their home-work before they pack their bags. The majority of travellers chronically underestimate their spend when they go on holiday. Thus, even if they have carefully pre-ordered money and avoided the worst of the rip-off charges, they end up having to visit ATMs anyhow and then fall prey to all the charges listed here. The other side to this is holidaymakers who over-estimate what they'll need, withdraw a wallet full of (very expensive) foreign currency and then return home having not spent it all. Not only will it leave them with a drawer filled with random notes bear-ing witness to holidays past, they'll also be paying handsomely for the memory. It has been estimated that UK travellers have hoarded £819m of leftover currency.[2]

One of the obvious ways to avoid at least some of the crip-pling charges is to withdraw larger amounts of cash less often. This would, of course, have negative security implications. You could also do some research to see if there are any free ATMs in the area you are visiting, although this won't let you avoid all the charges. Alternatively, you could look into some of the digi-tal solutions listed here.

Travel debit and credit cards

As a rule of thumb, using your existing, day-to-day credit and debit cards while travelling abroad is not a good idea. Even if you are conscientious and pay your credit card off in full as soon as you return, you'll still pay charges and, in some cases, a penalty fee every time your card comes out of your wallet to pay for something. However, all is not lost for fans of plastic over cash – there are some credit and debit cards that don't charge fees.

If you are weighing up this option, the first, perhaps most obvious, question is, credit or debit? Credit cards are generally easier to get, since you can apply for one anywhere, regardless of who you bank with. Debit cards are associated with individual accounts, so to get a new, non-fee paying one you may have to switch accounts, or certainly open a new account to run along-side your existing one. You have legal protection when you pay with credit cards, meaning the credit card provider is liable along with the retailer if anything goes wrong. Where credit cards are not such a winner is if you use them to withdraw cash when overseas. Most credit card providers charge fees or interest when you take out cash from an ATM abroad. Specialist overseas debit cards do not, meaning they can often work out more cheaply.

Best for: zero bank charges, card charges or top-up fees

If you want to avoid horrible bank charges when taking out money abroad, Starling Bank's debit card won't charge you a bean. You don't even need to switch your entire current account to the bank; you can simply set up an account and add some money into it before you travel. Unlike traditional accounts, *Starling* has no penalties for using your debit card abroad and no added ATM fees. Many foreign ATMs may well impose a fee, but it is possible to shop around and supermarkets often offer fee-free cash-back, just as they do in the UK. The exchange rates on the *Starling* MasterCard are in line with the globally accepted rates, and nothing is added on top. Also, unlike some prepaid travel cards, there is no charge to deliver the card or to top it up. The app is also really handy when it comes to tracking your day-to-day spending while you are abroad, because you will be able to use your phone to immediately see what you have spent, and where, as well as your remaining balance. So, if budgets are tight, you'll know when to ease off the spending so you don't run out of cash before you come home.

App for that: *Starling*

Best for: cashback travel credit

Digital challenger *Tandem* also boasts no fees for overseas spending via its MasterCard credit card. As well as fee-free spending, there is also the perk of an unlimited 0.5 per cent cashback on spending at home and abroad. Plus, there are no fees on purchases or on cash withdrawals in another currency. That said, it is wise to remember that it is not a good idea to take out cash on a credit card because you will still be charged interest even if you pay it off in full. *Tandem* charges 18.9 per cent on cash withdrawals, so the costs can spiral if you don't pay back what you owe quite fast. It works out at about £1.50 a month for each £100 withdrawn. You can minimize the cost of the interest by repaying the balance as soon as you can (you're only charged interest until you have fully repaid the balance). If you are likely to be reliant on a lot of trips to the cashpoint, this may not be the best option for you.

App for that: *Tandem*

Best for: convenience

Another interesting card to consider is *Curve*. This is an alternative for people who have wallets stuffed full of credit and debit cards that they feel they might wish to use as they travel. *Curve* gives you one card, which can stand in for any and all of those in your wallet, allowing you to lighten the load somewhat and only carry one piece of plastic with you. Obviously, it is not always an ideal scenario for a number of reasons, not least the security risk. If you lose your purse or wallet you will have lost *everything*. Plus, you will be subject to the charges listed at the beginning of the section. However, for those that really do want to spread the load over a number of cards, *Curve* lets you use all of your cards in just one card. You simply change to whichever one you want to use through the app that is linked to the card. The exchange rate on offer is the MasterCard one, however there is a flat 1 per cent fee on all transactions and it costs £35 to get a *Curve* card in the first place. International ATM withdrawals also incur a £2 fee.

App for that: *Curve*

Prepaid travel cards and swapping

Prepaid travel cards have long been a useful way to keep track of your travel spend. Simply load one up before you go abroad and then use it as you would a debit card, which is, of course, accepted in a vast number of hotels, restaurants, cafes and shops. Obviously, you can't spend more than you have loaded onto a prepaid card, so it is a really helpful budgeting tool that stops you slipping into the red. Plus, they are a useful fraud deterrent, since if anyone did get hold of someone's prepaid card details, they wouldn't be able to run up a huge bill at the cardholder's expense. Also, if it is lost or stolen, the cardholder can simply contact the provider and get it blocked. This way they won't lose any money at all, although there may be a need to pay up to £10 for a new card.

Although using prepaid cards is a very similar experience to using your credit or debit card as you travel, there are differences. For example, the exchange rate is usually locked in on the day you load up a prepaid card. When you use your usual plastic, the exchange rate is calculated at the time you make the purchase. This can, of course, be a plus or a minus. If your domestic currency suddenly strengthens when you are away, you'll find yourself worse off as you make your purchases with a prepaid card, certainly compared to people who are paying the on-the-spot exchange rate. It does, of course, work the other way around too.

As always, it is well worth shopping around, and I'd advise anyone to take some time to compare the various prepaid cards on offer, since exchange rates do vary. Some cards use the spot rate, which is the usual exchange rate, while others look to MasterCard or Visa's version, while others will pick one of these two and then add a certain percentage as their exchange fee. This can be around 1 per cent to 2.5 per cent. It should also be noted that some prepaids charge ATM withdrawal fees and others have low limits on what the cardholder is allowed to take out each month. Also, if you are planning to hire a car, there are some places that do not accept any cards that do not have the hirer's name on it. This doesn't happen everywhere, but it can add a layer of anxiety to a trip, which is a drawback if you are the type of traveller that gets stressed out by uncertainty.

Almost all prepaid cards are linked to an app, so you can monitor your spending and load more money onto the card as you need it. If your destination is a country with bad internet or patchy coverage, you may want to be sure you have loaded up enough money on your card before you leave.

Best for: fair prepaid rates with peer-to-peer

An innovative idea in prepaids is the *WeSwap* app, which is a peer-to-peer currency exchange that cuts out the middleman completely and therefore boasts that it offers the best possible exchange rate. *WeSwap* uses their online community to exchange currencies with other travellers who are heading in the opposite direction and want to get rid of one currency for another. By swapping money between users, it tries to avoid buying foreign currency from banks. After setting up an account online and entering a destination, users are sent a prepaid MasterCard linked to the *WeSwap* account. Simply load on the funds you want to swap and you'll be matched with people who want to exchange in the opposite way. Once you are matched, your account will be loaded with the new currency and you can spend your funds using a prepaid card. It's free to use in ATMs too. You can make up to two withdrawals a day as long as you withdraw more than US $200 or 200 euros, so it pays to make a smaller number of large withdrawals while you are abroad. Otherwise you'll be charged a fee of US $2.25 or 1.75 euros. For the first six months that you have the card, you pay no exchange fees and also get the interbank rate. However, you do have to wait seven days between swapping your money to being able to access your foreign currency, unless you pay a fee. After six months there is a 1 per cent exchange fee for seven-day transfers. You can avoid fees completely if you can get five friends to sign up to *WeSwap*.

Again, there is the option to convert any unused currency to your domestic version, and *weswapbuyback.com* also invites people to gather up all the random dollars, yen or rupee notes (not coins) that they may have tucked away in their drawers and send them through the post to be credited to their *WeSwap* account within three days. Or, if you choose, the sum can be donated to charity. The exchange rate on offer is 1 per cent to 2 per cent for major currencies and slightly more for exotic ones. The app doesn't accept *all* currencies, but the service will warn you at the order stage if a particular request can't be met.

App for that: *WeSwap*

Sending money abroad

What though, if you are not the person requiring the cash to spend in some far-off clime? Maybe your gap-year son or daughter miscalculated their budget and needs an urgent top-up, or you are working abroad and want to send cash home to family. In the past, bank charges have been as high as £25 per transfer to an international bank, which is not only a bit of a rip-off but also prohibitively expensive. The fees are also incurred on both sides too, so the sender and the recipient both pay. This is not to mention the occasional somewhat sneaky practice of hiding the true amount that is actually being charged. While some financial providers offer 'fee-free' rates, they adjust the exchange rate to make up for the loss or introduce myriad small charges to disguise the true cost. Whichever way you cut it, it can be pretty frustrating because there is nothing worse than losing a chunk of your cash during the transfer process.

Fortunately, the tide has shifted, and there are now lots of cheaper alternatives out there. Indeed, there are quite a wide range of options emerging, so it's worth looking around to find the one that best suits your particular needs.

Best for: ease of use

To begin with, I am bound to mention *Starling* once again. You can use the banking app to transfer money abroad, and its exchange rates and fees beat all the major banks. A sum of 0.4 per cent is added to the transaction, which is taken from the conversion amount. It is completely fair and transparent too, with the in-app currency calculator displaying exactly how much you are spending before you click 'go'. At the time of writing, this service is available to send money to 39 countries in 21 currencies.

App for that: *Starling*

Best for: one-off or small payments

There are a number of specialized online services that are useful for sending one-off small payments from as little as £1. This can be handy when paying for goods bought from eBay, or to send a gift to a family member overseas. Payment is made via your domestic currency, usually via internet transfer, which is then converted and sent to the receiving bank abroad in about two to four working days. *Azimo* is one such service that allows you to send money to over 190 countries. Fees start from £1, £12 for SWIFT payments (direct bank-to-bank transfer that makes sure your international payment is delivered speedily) and £1 for mobile top-ups. The app has a useful tracking feature, with a full money back guarantee if something goes wrong with the transfer. This can be quite reassuring for someone concerned about using a service like this for the first time. There is a lucrative refer-a-friend scheme, which pays £10 per person you invite and an extra £25 when you invite a trio.

One of *Azimo*'s most interesting features is that it allows you to send and request money both in the UK and overseas using just a mobile number. If money is being sent to a person without an *Azimo* app themselves, they will get a message with a link to download it. Then, all they have to do is to fill in their bank details to withdraw the funds. Once set up, their details will be saved and the next transfer will be instant.

Circle offers a similar service, *CirclePay*, which imports your contact list and lets you open up a chat with whomever you are planning to send money to. You can even jazz up the discussion with emoji and gifs if you are so inclined. Simply link a debit card or bank account to the app for instant transfers. The app is free to download on Android and Apple devices and *Circle* promises no fees to users, instead charging a model market exchange rate.

Apps for that: *Azimo, Circle*

Best for: wearable app

If you love your gadgets, the money transfer app for you is most likely *WorldFirst*. Not only is it available as an app, but it is also set up to work via Android and Apple smart watches. The company boasts that those with wearable technology can make transfers with just 'five taps and three swipes'. It is not all about gimmicks though. *WorldFirst* offers a useful 'rate alert' feature that helps make sure you only transfer cash when the rate is at its best. This service is set up for transferring larger amounts of money: there is a minimum transfer threshold of £1,000. It also requires more information to set up than the services detailed in the subsection before. It does reward the user with a conversion tool displaying the latest inter-bank rate, live rate graphs and links to market news and exchange rate analysis.

App for that: *WorldFirst*

Best for: cheapest money guarantee

Another interesting money transfer service is *TransferWise*, which doesn't really transfer cash at all. It simply matches the person wanting to send money abroad with other people in other countries who want to move their cash in the opposite direction. Say, for example, you wanted to send US $1,000 to someone in Canada. Rather than actually physically despatching US $1,000 to Canada, *TransferWise* just adds the US $1,000 you send them to its pot of US dollars and pays the recipient the equivalent amount of Canadian dollars out of their Canadian pot. The peer-to-peer service has a large store of different currencies in its bank accounts all over the world, and since much of the legwork is taken out of the transaction they're able to offer a much keener exchange rate. *TransferWise* accepts transfer orders for amounts ranging from £1 to £1 million at the bank rate and charges a flat fee of 0.5 per cent on any value transferred through the service.

One of the main pros of this service is it is very easy to use, since all the complexity of a peer-to-peer transaction is taken care of in the app. For an added layer of customer satisfaction it also features a 'cheapest money guarantee'. If a customer receives a better quote from another provider, *TransferWise* undertakes to either match it or refund the difference. The service supports more than 27 currencies around the world, including the market's largest parings such as US dollars, British pounds, euros, Indian rupees, Japanese yen and Australian dollars.

The potential downsides are minimal. In fact, the only one to note is that the transfer process is not immediate and most exchanges take anywhere from one to four days, depending on the currencies involved.

Recently *TransferWise* has made the whole process even slicker by offering a 'borderless account' that provides a debit card to make funds available easily anywhere in the world and account numbers in several countries for receiving payments.

App for that: *TransferWise*

Fly now, pay later

Paying for a big holiday nearly always represents a huge financial commitment. It's actually quite surprising that the concept of paying for travel in instalments is largely unheard of in the United States, Europe and South Africa, although it is quite common in many other countries. Chances are though, the practice may begin to become more widespread, certainly if the number of fintechs eyeing the space are anything to go by.

Paying for travel in instalments has a lot of potential advantages. Imagine, for example, you spend months and months making sacrifices and saving hard, all the while dreaming of your much-deserved holiday. Then, just as you get close to your target sum, you discover that prices have risen and your flights are out of reach. Or, say, you are compelled to take an unexpected trip. The chances are you will face being out of pocket for months thanks to the unbudgeted for, last-minute purchase, or may get stuck with a costly loan. Paying by instalments reduces the risk and creates much more certainty about what you are buying and when.

Best for: ease of use

Flight buying platform *Flymble*'s mantra is that access to travel should be no different than paying off your mobile phone, a new sofa or catalogue shopping. It is comparatively simple to use too. Decide where you want to go, search for a flight on the *Flymble* website, fill in your details and pass a speedy credit check. The cost includes a small service fee, which is payable up front, as part of the initial down payment. After that, the price quoted at the checkout is the price that is paid with no additional charges or nasty interest fees added on. Travellers can choose between paying over 3, 6 or 10-month instalments.

App for that: *Flymble*

Best for: choice

Affirm has linked with travel giant Expedia's US site to enable instalment payments on a range of travel products, from flights to accommodation. To find the feature, select the 'monthly payments' tab and choose between options to pay over 3, 6 or 12 months using bank transfer or debit card, with an APR of between 10 per cent to 30 per cent. It is early days in the trial, but where Expedia goes the rest of the travel industry generally follows. It seems inevitable that other airlines, hotel chains and travel search companies will be watching closely.

Another one to keep an eye on is *Airfordable*, which uses risk assessment software as an alternative to doing credit checks. The idea behind it is to make the process more efficient. It may also keep the costs down too. *Airfordable* charges between 10 and 20 per cent of the ticket price as a fee and then automatically sets up a repayment plan so the flight is paid for before the date of travel. It works with all the major US travel providers such as Expedia, Priceline and Google Flights. Customers simply take a screen shot of an itinerary, submit the trip details and then place a deposit on the overall cost. Regular payments can be made on the overall balance and then, when the loan is paid off in full, the ticket is confirmed and sent to the traveller.

Apps for that: *Affirm*, *Airfordable*

Best for: social savings

South African fintech *FOMOTravel*, or 'fear of missing out', is an instalment plan with a difference. Like other such plans it requires recurring monthly payments to cover the cost of travel, however in this case there is a facility for users to invite friends and family to contribute to the payments. This could be very effective when 'crowdfunding' big travel experiences such as a honeymoon. There are incentives too, if a customer shares their trip on social media.

App for that: *FOMOTravel*

Notes

1   Mintel [accessed 31 March 2018] Travel Money UK [Online] http://academic.mintel.com/display/858899/
2   WeSwap website: www.weswap.com

CHAPTER FOURTEEN

Borrow clever

Traditionally, the loan model has been based on a tried and tested format: banks and credit unions accept deposits of money from some customers and use the capital to extend loans to other customers. To make money out of the process, they charged the borrowers more interest than they paid out to the savers. The concept has always been OK, as far as it went, although the deals were not always something to shout about.

One of the most common complaints about loans comes from the borrower's side. It centres around the many hoops that would-be borrowers have to jump through before getting their hands on any cash. They have a point too: the process has been anything but consumer friendly, with customers compelled to fill out long forms, provide all sorts of supporting documentation and then often having to wait weeks for a response. Even then, some deserving borrowers slip through the net and get locked out of the mainstream lending market even though they really should be considered a good bet. It's easy to fall through the gaps when lenders use general data as a reference point and rely on traditional credit scoring metrics to assess loan applications. The response from lenders is that they (understandably) need to do their utmost to prevent the risk of defaults.

Thanks to the proliferation of real-time data available about each and every one of us, there is now an opportunity for fintechs to fill in the gaps and make the process work better for everyone. For a start, fintechs can use technology to vastly cut down on the paperwork required. The basis for lending to each individual can also be more easily scrutinized and the whole process is much, much quicker. Fully digitizing loans also brings greater transparency. As I have said many times in this book, it is so much better if finances are not treated at arm's length with an out-of-sight-out-of-mind attitude. Using the available technology means borrowers will have constant visibility around the full cost of loans, tracking repayments and other useful information, so there are never any surprises.

It was a boom in peer-to peer-lending, which began in 2005 with firms such as *Zopa*, that heralded the first signs of change in the loan market. This is where groups of individuals are matched together to organize personal loans, with the business that organizes the partnership pocketing a small fee for the connection. But, progress and change haven't stopped there. Fintechs are now tackling every sort of debt, from student loans, to mortgages, to lines of credit for business. In each case the starting point has been: is there an easier and cheaper way of doing things that will also open up the market to people who might once have been excluded from getting finance? (Or certainly found the process off-puttingly slow and cumbersome.) Once again, technology is at the centre of these new solutions and the lending services that have emerged as a result of these changes offer something that was previously unavailable – namely a faster, simpler application process, followed by a rapid move through to approval and borrowers actually receiving funds in their accounts. Digital processes are particularly effective in the loans market because this is where having access to all the available data and connecting the dots really comes into its own, with the critical importance of speed and accuracy of decision-making. Previously, when it was just down to humans making all the checks, things frequently ground to a halt, or at least slowed down considerably. Automating the assessment of the various risks not only speeds things up but also offers the advantage of lowering operating costs, which can translate into more competitive loans for consumers.

Peer-to-peer lending

One of the many far-reaching consequences of the global financial crisis of 2008 was that the banks stopped lending. Burned by the excesses of the previous era, and with books full of toxic loans and mortgage securities to unravel, high street lenders became completely risk adverse. When customers asked for loans, they invariably found the door firmly closed. The situation presented the ideal environment for the then fledgling peer-to-peer lending (P2P) practice to flourish.

The mechanics behind P2P are simple and operate rather like an online matchmaker. Individuals looking to borrow sums are matched with savers who are willing to put money aside for a longer period in exchange for a decent return. Since the banking middleman is cut out of the mix, borrowers can get slightly lower interest rates than they'd normally be offered on the high street, while lenders get better headline rates. Meanwhile, the P2P matchmaker takes a fee for the introduction.

From a borrower and a lender point of view, there are many advantages over and above receiving better interest rates. Borrowers benefit from an easy, swift online application and approvals process. The interest rates, which are lower than those offered by traditional financial institutions and credit cards, are fixed, with no hidden fees. There are no prepayment penalties if you decide to pay off the loan before the due date, and loans are unsecured so borrowers don't need to provide collateral, such as the title to their house or car.

The lending side is interesting too. For a start, it opens up an entirely new investment opportunity to people who may never have considered lending as a way to grow their savings. Lenders have the potential to earn far more via P2P lending than if they'd simply stuck their money in a savings account. There are a range of options, from very small to very large investments, and lenders can even spread the risk by investing in a portfolio of hundreds, even thousands, of loans. Risk can also be further spread by lending across all sorts of different sectors and applications. In return for investment, lenders receive a monthly repayment of the principal sum as well as interest, as borrowers repay their dues. They can choose to withdraw the repaid funds altogether or to reinvest the payments in further P2P loans.

The P2P lending market has flourished since the late 2000s. When *Zopa*, the first lending platform, was launched in 2005, loans totalled £1.5 million. Today, there has been more than £10 billion loaned in the UK alone.[1] Globally, the P2P lending market is forecast to reach £688 billion by the year 2024.[2] P2P start-ups have taken advantage of the most up-to-date technology to build their systems, which is again something that gives them a competitive advantage over traditional lenders, most of which rely on clunky, outdated systems that provide a relatively slow service to customers. This is not to say every P2P application is not carefully assessed. Each borrower is subject to the same stringent credit checks and rated according to risk – technology simply speeds the process up and makes it more efficient. Online platforms also automate much of the legal and regulatory processes involved in lending. Borrowers in need of quick access to capital can get decisions swiftly. In many cases funds can even be raised on the same day as the application.

So, you may well be asking, a better interest rate, a quicker decision and an altogether more efficient system; what is the downside? Well, there are risks for both borrowers and lenders and it may not be the right option for everyone. If, for example, a would-be borrower does not have a brilliant credit rating, the P2P loan that they secure may well come with a prohibitively high interest rate to help mitigate against the greater chance of default. If the borrower takes up the offer, they will be stuck with this high interest rate for months and years to come. In this case, there is a strong argument for the potential borrower waiting a while and taking measures to improve their credit rating before applying for a loan. Alternatively, if an applicant is looking to borrow a lot of money, they may find it difficult to find a lender as it is not always possible to borrow significant amounts in this way.

There is arguably more to consider if you are coming at P2P from the lending side. After all, it is your nest egg that is potentially at risk. One of the most obvious potential downsides is that your capital sum may not be repaid. While P2P has worked exceedingly well for many, returns, and indeed the recovery of your initial sum, are not guaranteed. On the plus side though, P2P businesses are now regulated. In the UK, for example, the Financial Conduct Authority began to regulate them in April 2014. Its rules clearly state that P2P firms must present information clearly, be transparent about potential risks and have plans in place should anything go wrong. Any P2P firm that doesn't follow the rules risks sanctions and large fines. In addition, they must have at least £50,000 in capital (more for larger firms) that is available in the case of financial difficulties.

It is worth noting that while the industry is better regulated, it doesn't have the protection of the Financial Services Compensation Scheme. This is the safety net offered to all savers in the UK, which guarantees to pay out up to £85,000 per person, per financial institution, in the event that the holder of their funds goes bust. If you lent your money via a P2P firm that subsequently went out of business, the onus would be on you to collect what you were owed. While the P2P specialist should have insurance to ease things in such an eventuality, there are no guarantees of a smooth outcome.

There have also been murmurs of discontent among financial commentators that the P2P industry has expanded too quickly and aggressively by exploiting the weaknesses of traditional banks that have not been quite so fleet of foot. P2P firms have certainly taken full advantage of the prolonged period of low interest rates. As interest rates inevitably start to rise, investors may have less incentive to seek out 'higher risk' areas such as P2P. All this comes at a time when there is evidence that the interest rates offered by P2P platforms are already not as comparatively attractive as they used to be. If the interest rate gap narrows to match that offered by more 'mainstream' lenders, it has been speculated that P2P firms may gravitate towards picking up loan business at the riskier end of things, among those with low or no credit ratings. This would certainly be riskier for investors and could have a damaging long-term effect on the growth of P2P.

For savers in the UK, many of the P2P companies now offer ISA accounts as well, so you can save an amount tax free and even use them in place of traditional banks and investment providers for your yearly ISA allowance.

As with every area of financial services, there are always risks. The best way to mitigate the risks is to understand what you are dealing with and become fully informed.

Best for: established track record

As one of the first P2P players, *Zopa* remains one of the most established and has gained a good foothold among borrowers looking for personal loans. If you decide to become a lender, *Zopa* splits up the amount being invested into £10 chunks, which are then spread evenly across many different loans. Lenders are, therefore, exposed to a diverse range of borrowers, which are classified from A* to E, and this has the advantage that they don't place all their P2P (nest) eggs in one basket. Investors, who can invest as little as £10 with no upper limit, can chose from two different products, *Zopa Core* and *Zopa Plus*, which offer different levels of risk and return. While *Zopa* once offered rates of between 5 and 6 per cent, after bad debts and fees, investors are now earning between 4.5 per cent and 5.2 per cent. That said, it is still a decent rate and the rate offered has *Zopa*'s assumed bad debt and fee deducted, so an expected number of loan defaults are already factored in. Lenders are able to withdraw funds early, but there is a fee of 1 per cent of the total amount to pay.

On the other side of the fence, borrowers must be at least 20 years old and have a good visible credit history. The minimum lend amount is £1,000 and the maximum level is £25,000. The borrowing term is from one to five years, but there are no penalties for early settlement. If a borrower fails to make a payment, they will receive a call from a *Zopa* representative and 70 per cent of the time the borrower will clear the debt within a few days. After 30 days of arrears, there will be discussions to determine whether the borrower needs help and new arrangements may be made, however debt collection agencies may also get involved.

Not far behind *Zopa* in the head-start stakes is *LendingClub*, which was founded in 2006 and is headquartered in California. *LendingClub* claims to be the world's largest P2P lending platform with billions of dollars in loans going through its books. It is easy to see why, since it boasts returns of 8 per cent. Borrowers need to reach a minimum credit rating threshold score to apply, and over two-thirds of loan applications get rejected, thanks to the risk management performed by *LendingClub*. Borrowers choose between a minimum loan of US $1,000 and a maximum of US $40,000, which can be repaid over three to five years. Those with good credit scores can get interest rates as low as 6.95 per cent, however those with poor credit ratings can see rates as high as 35.89 per cent. The interest rate is fixed for the term of the loan. Loans are available for both individuals and small businesses.

The process of signing up as an investor is simple and takes a few minutes to complete online, however there are minimum net worth and income requirements, and an initial deposit of US $1,000 is needed to get started. Lenders can choose between manually picking their investments to build up their portfolio of loans, or leaving it to an automated process. *LendingClub* charges an annual fee of 1 per cent per loan note held within their marketplace.

Apps for that: *Zopa, LendingClub*

Best for: ease of use

One of the main goals of *Ratesetter* is to make P2P investing as simple as possible. Indeed, some reviewers have said the experience for investors is almost as simple as putting cash into a savings account, although it is, of course, an investment not a savings product. The returns are also better, which is what you'd expect in return for taking on a greater risk.

Lenders' money is automatically allocated to borrowers, which is different to some P2P providers who allow lenders a more active role in choosing who they lend to. *Ratesetter* aims to cover any late payments automatically through a compensation fund.

The minimum lend is just £10 for a term of one or five years, or on a rolling basis. In other words, once repaid, lenders simply reinvest. Lenders can expect average rates of return of around 3 per cent for the rolling market, 3.7 per cent for one year and 5.9 per cent for five years.

Borrowers are subject to a minimum borrowing amount of £500 and a maximum of £35,000, depending upon personal circumstances. Borrowing terms are between six months to five years and, again, there are no early penalties for paying the loan off early.

If you would like to have a bit more of a say over where your money goes, *Funding Circle* might be a good alternative. Here, interested investors can pick and choose where they put their money, but others can happily use *Funding Circle*'s Autobid feature, which automatically allocates investments across 100 businesses. Investors must put in at least £2,000 to meet the minimum £20 investment requirements towards individual companies. There is no provision fund with this service, which was launched in 2010, so there is a bigger risk of losing money if borrowers don't come through with repayments. However, the upside is that the potential rates of return are higher and *Funding Circle* claims that no one who has lent money in this way has lost money. If choosing your own lending picks, the advice is to allocate the smallest amount possible across the widest range of borrowers to spread the risk. *Funding Circle* has operations in the UK, United States, Germany, Spain and the Netherlands. The minimum amount threshold for borrowers is £5,000, with a £1 million maximum, on a borrowing term of six months to five years. The average rate of return for lenders is 6.5 per cent on A+ grade loans.

Apps for that: *Ratesetter, Funding Circle*

Best for: spreading the risk

Frequently cited as one of the United States' fastest growing companies, facilitating over US $10 billion in personal loans to date, *Prosper*'s model focusses on the most common risk in P2P, namely that borrowers fail to repay their loans. The loans on offer are unsecured, and without a house or car at stake, borrowers are more likely to default (although it would subsequently affect their credit score). *Prosper*'s solution is to encourage investors to diversify with enough loans to spread the risk of any default thinly enough so that it barely impacts on the return. It should also be said that *Prosper* does not simply lend to anyone with a pulse. Applicants need to reach a FICO credit rating threshold of 640 or higher and clearly state the purpose of the loan in their application.

Borrowers can apply for loans from US $2,000 to US $35,000 and are rated from AA, which is lower risk, all the way through A to E, and then on to HR, or high risk. The higher the risk, the higher the interest rate they pay. Previous *Prosper* borrowers with a good loan history may be offered a lower APR since they are statistically less likely to default.

Investors put a small, US $25 portion, into each loan pot, which is known as a note. Thus, with a single lump sum of US $5,000, they could get 200 notes. If one of the 200 borrowers defaults, the lender would lose 1/200 of his or her investment, or 0.5 per cent. *Prosper* borrowers typically have an interest rate of 14 per cent on their loans and around 4 or 5 per cent is lost to defaulters. After a 1 per cent fee is paid, this means an investor earns 8 per cent (14 per cent interest rate – 6 per cent defaults/fees = 8 per cent). The most obvious risk is, of course, that the default rate could rise, if for example there is an economic downturn and unemployment rates rise significantly.

App for that: *Prosper*

Small business loans

A significant advantage to the new fintech loan models is that they open up access to borrowing to a much wider range of people. Would-be borrowers who might have previously struggled to find a lender are now more likely to be able to find one that is willing to put up cash. This is particularly useful for small businesses that now find themselves with easier and quicker access to capital and lines of credit without having to put up their homes as collateral, or source guarantees from friends and family. This is not to say fintechs are loaning out money willy-nilly. It is simply that these firms are taking full advantage of flexible and comprehensive scoring algorithms that use big data and AI for a more accurate view of a borrower's creditworthiness. Traditional banks are just not set up to do this, since their scoring models tend to largely be based on a one-size-fits-all model. They are certainly not geared towards effective analysis of specific sectors such as small- and medium-sized enterprises (SMEs).

Best for: online retailers

Although US-based fintech *Kabbage* uses many of the traditional sources of banking data to assess SME loans, it also utilizes a wealth of other information to help it in its swift assessment of borrowers. The service, which really suits small online retailers that may need to invest in stock as they scale up their businesses, or small businesses that need a boost to working capital to cover day-to-day expenses, uses anything from bank account records, to historic shipping data for the products or services being sold, to data from e-commerce platforms such as Etsy or eBay, to social media. It all goes into the mix and is used to analyse the risk. And the best part about it? While in the past it has taken some traditional banks weeks to weigh up whether to lend, *Kabbage* aims to make decisions in just seven minutes.

To apply for a *Kabbage* loan, the business borrowing the money must be at least a year old, with an annual turnover in excess of US $50,000 or revenue of US $4,200 a month for the last three months. While the loan period is for 6 to 12 months, borrowers are strongly encouraged to pay back their loans in a smaller time frame. To underline this stance, there are no early payment fees and the firm's online tools show how much borrowers will save in fees if they pay it all back within, say, four months, rather than six.

The fintech itself sets the size of the loan, rather than the borrower requesting a specific amount. *Kabbage*'s offer, which can range from US $500 to US $250,000, is based on its assessment of the business and its turnover. The borrower doesn't need to take the entire sum in one go. They can draw down one loan amount and then return at a later date to take more, provided it is within the scope of the original loan offer. There is a downside though: the interest rates being quoted are among the highest on the market, so any business would be advised to avoid using these loans for large capital expenditure. Anything like that would be better financed through a long-term, lower-cost loan.

App for that: *Kabbage*

Best for: flexibility

Square started life as a simple gadget that plugged into smart phones and allowed small traders to accept payment cards. It was the brainchild of Twitter founder Jack Dorsey and his friend Jim McKelvey who were seeking a solution to the issue of why it was so difficult for SMEs to accept plastic from their customers, which put them at an instant disadvantage to larger retailers. At the time, only 30 to 40 per cent of small traders who wanted to set up a system to process card payments were accepted by banks. *Square*'s intervention managed to get that rate up to 99 per cent. The pair quickly realized that the simple square card reader they devised also had another significant application thanks to the wealth of data it collected from each vendor. *Square Capital* was launched to lend capital to *Square* customers. After a period of analysing card receipts, the algorithm sends customers the offer of an appropriately sized loan. The funds are available from the next working day and the loan is repaid via card receipts. *Square* bases the repayment terms of its working capital loans on a percentage of a business's daily credit card sales processed through *Square*. No hard credit score checks are required because the credit card sales totals tell the lender all it needs to know about how much customers are spending with the business in question. The loans are quite small, typically around US $6,000, and therefore less than a traditional bank would generally bother with. However, the capital sums are undoubtedly useful for smaller businesses and, indeed, many larger businesses are starting to use the service.

PayPal's working capital loan service works in a similar way. Businesses are only eligible for a *PayPal* loan if they already process payments with *PayPal* and reach a certain threshold in sales. It's possible to borrow up to 25 per cent of annual *PayPal* sales and there is no interest rate. *PayPal* charges a fixed fee based on *PayPal* sales volume, account history, the amount of the loan and the percentage of sales put towards repayment.

SmartBiz offers an interest rate ranging from an APR of 9 per cent to 11 per cent on loans ranging from US $30,000 to US $350,000. A really high credit score is not a requirement, but an applicant's credit rating still needs to be good. Any business seeking funds also needs to be well established, with at least three years' trading under its belt and minimum annual revenues of US $100,000 plus, depending upon the size of loan required. To apply, a business must provide *SmartBiz* with copies of its tax returns, which are used to analyse its financial health. Further financial data required includes current income, bank balances and details of outstanding loans. The AI-driven assessment service is designed to help applicants by showing how banks view their business and offers suggestions on how to improve finances if they don't reach approval levels, or Loan Ready Score, as it is called. *SmartBiz* charges slightly higher fees than a traditional bank, taking a 4 per cent cut from an approved loan to cover 'referral and packaging fees', but the interest rates are relatively low.

Apps for that: *Square*, *PayPal*, *SmartBiz*

Best for: factoring

There is an estimated US $40 trillion globally in outstanding invoices at any point in time and an extended wait for payment can be agony for some businesses. Small businesses are frequently the most vulnerable, and working capital is an ever-present bugbear for many SMEs. It is no surprise therefore that many turn to invoice factoring firms to improve cash flow. Factoring (or invoice finance) is the process whereby a business sells its unpaid bills, or invoices, to a finance company in return for a cash advance. The advance can be up to 80 per cent of the invoice's face value, and the cash is usually received within 24 to 48 hours. The small business gets the money when it needs it, leaving a potentially greater sum for the factoring company to collect a little further down the line but with the risk and the pain of collection belonging now to the factoring company.

Kansas City based *C2FO* is a similar idea. The concept is fairly simple. Indeed, it is based on one that has been around for a while: a discount is offered to partners who pay on time. However, where *C2FO* differs is it is an online marketplace where companies with cash who are willing and able to pay their invoices early can work together with suppliers who need that cash. In this digital tool, a customer adds a firm's approved invoices to *C2FO* and that firm can request early payment at a discounted rate. When the offer is accepted, the customer will pay the business direct, often within 24 hours. The business in question doesn't need to offer up all of its invoices for early payment. It can pick and choose, and it also has control over the rate of discount being offered. What makes it an attractive option is it is extremely easy to set up and manage, and suppliers do not have to pay any fees. They are simply offered an attractive discount to speed up the payment process.

Three further rivals in the factoring space are US company *Fundbox* and European services *Marketinvoice* and *Frenns*. *Fundbox* and *Marketinvoice* provide short-term loans to businesses while they wait for invoices to be settled. *Fundbox* plugs into a business's accounting software and analyses a variety of data points to judge a risk profile. Since there are two sides to the settlement of invoices, *Fundbox* also takes into account the firm being invoiced and any risk on that side. The service boasts that it takes just 15 seconds to create an account and 50 seconds for *Fundbox* to underwrite an invoice. Customers get their money the next working day and are rewarded for repaying the loan before the invoice is due.

Frenns is a fully automated process that uses AI to factor invoices for European SMEs. The process is synchronized with a business's usual online accounting systems, after which *Frenns* processes them and puts them up for auction. Investors are free to place bids on them and the company issuing the auction is free to choose the bid that offers the most competitive interest rate and time frame. Once the auction is closed, up to 99 per cent of the invoice is advanced, often within an hour, with the remaining capital being withheld to cover commission and bank transfer fees.

Apps for that: *Fundbox*, *Marketinvoice*, *Frenns*

Best for: businesses/individuals with little or no credit history

According to the World Bank, nearly 60 per cent of adults in Sub-Saharan Africa and nearly 45 per cent in developing countries are either unbanked or severely underbanked. This makes it really difficult for them to access loans because lenders have next to no data on the potential borrowers. The result: up to 2.5 billion people are unable to access funds that could very well help lift them and indeed whole communities out of poverty. For years it has been a vicious circle, since without the ability to source loans any hopes of progress are inevitably brought to a sharp halt. Today, the explosion in smart phone ownership has transformed the situation. The medium is the perfect, user-friendly vehicle to offer easy access to funds, and it also provides an efficient way for people to search the availability of new services. It's win-win for everyone, since the technology streamlines the process, which in turns keeps costs down.

Tala uses mobile phone data to get a better sense of the would-be borrower and can collect over 10,000 unique data points per user, scrutinizing everything from social media accounts to their web search history. The idea is to get a sense of the 'financial identity' of the person behind that data, rather than just the bare numbers. For example, social media shows a lot about a person's underlying identity and the friends a person associates with. If those friends have already repaid loans, that is a positive sign. Similarly, social media will flag up if someone spends a large amount of time socializing and drinking alcohol with friends, rather than working, which is not a positive indication of the likelihood of a loan being repaid. Most of *Tala*'s current users are in Kenya, although *Tala* has now also expanded elsewhere into the Philippines, Nigeria and Tanzania and is eyeing India and Mexico.

Also of note is *Kreditech*, which provides access to working capital in emerging markets, so borrowers can purchase inventory, make short-term investments and bridge cash flow gaps.

In Europe, *Iwoca* (or Instant Working Capital) uses technology to assess small businesses on their trading data, via thousands of data points, rather than simply through a credit score. Flexible credit is offered from £1,000, with the limit and interest rate depending on the business's performance. Funds can be available within four hours of application.

Apps for that: *Tala*, *Kreditech*, *Iwoca*

Other loans

Best for: online purchases

The idea of store charge cards has been around for more than a century after a handful of US department stores and oil companies decided to ease the way for customers (and keep them loyal) by setting up their own unique cards that were only ever accepted at the issuing merchant. The idea really took off in 1946, when the Charg-It card appeared. The bank behind Charg-It reimbursed merchants for any sale made and then recouped the sum from the customer after that. *Affirm* is the modern fintech equivalent of this idea. Founded by Max Levchin, who was also co-founder of *PayPal*, which was one of the earliest digital payment companies to be launched, this new offering finances the purchases of online retail customers via instant loans. Customers simply make their purchases and select *Affirm* at the checkout, after which *Affirm* settles the full amount with the store and then recoups the loan in instalments from the customer. At launch the app partnered with more than 150 online merchants in the United States, including ones that offer travel, furniture, phones and fitness, and interest rates typically range from 10 per cent to 30 per cent. Borrowers have up to one year to repay the sum.

Affirm's service has been expanded to include a mobile app, which has been likened to a 'virtual credit card'. This app can be used like a line of credit for pretty much any online purchase. The virtual card grants the user a one-time card number for a specific online purchase, and an expiry date and a three-digit number. The subsequent repayment plan is managed through the app.

There are no late fees or prepayment fees for the service, as the costs are recouped through the interest rates. Therefore, the longer you take to repay the loan, the more you will pay. Unlike many lenders or credit cards, *Affirm* performs a 'soft pull' on your credit, which means the inquiry won't be listed on your report. It is also possible to improve your credit rating using the service, since your positive repayment history is reported to credit bureau Experian.

Credit is only extended for the item being bought. *Affirm* says it will turn down loans if it detects excessive borrowings.

App for that: *Affirm*

Best for: student loans

In the UK, students have mostly resorted to the government-owned Student Loans Company to finance the £9,250 a year tuition fees due to universities. This is because banks are generally unwilling to advance the cash required for the duration of the three- or four-year university course to those with little or no credit history and no financial support from family. Interest rates, which are linked to the RPI measure of inflation, can be eye-wateringly high and begin accruing from the moment the loan is taken out.

It is hardly surprising that this sector has come under the gaze of fintechs since there is a clear gap in the market to provide students with low-cost loans to help fund them through their studies. *Future Finance* is a start-up that specializes in providing loans of £2,000 to £40,000 to students in higher education in the UK. Rates vary from 11.9 per cent to 25 per cent APR and are calculated according to future earning potential. Thus the application process takes into account personal circumstances, the university being attended and choice of degree course as much as any credit history. The debts are tailored so borrowers can make lower monthly repayments while studying and are kept lower for a further three months on graduation as students get settled into their chosen career.

Another lender is *Prodigy Finance*, which assesses students through a predictive scorecard that uses data about a student's academic background to predict future earnings. The platform specializes in loans for international post-graduate students, particularly those who have secured places on selected Master's courses at the top 100 globally ranked universities.

While not strictly a student loan, *Grant Fairy* is well worth a mention in this section on financing studies. This mobile app matches students with thousands of scholarships, bursaries and grants to help towards university tuition fees provided by UK universities, foundations and organizations. There is a £4.99 monthly fee or a £23.99 annual fee to access the comprehensive database of funding options. It offers personalized scholarship searches as well as daily scholarship updates from organizations such as the Bank of England and the Vegetarian Society. It is even possible to set application deadline reminders.

In the United States, where student debt totals US $1.5 trillion, with over 44 million Americans still holding student debt, *SoFi* offers what it claims is a more 'holistic' approach to paying off these large sums. It encourages students to refinance their debts and says they can save over US $20,000 by doing so. Classified as a non-traditional lender ie it doesn't operate like a bank, *SoFi* offers a range of fixed and variable rate payment plans. Applicants are asked to fill in an online or smartphone form, with their details of their education and basic employment history. Unlike most loan firms, *SoFi* does not check credit scores so there is no hard pull on credit ratings. To qualify, borrowers need to be at least 18 years old, have graduated from eligible universities and be employed, or holding a job offer with a start date within 90 days. There also needs to be a reasonable financial history behind them.

Benefits of a *SoFi* student loan go beyond the simple finance. Also on offer is career support, an Entrepreneur Program and regular member events across the United States. In addition, there is unemployment protection, should the borrower lose their job, where payments can be paused. *SoFi* even says it will help the borrower in their search for a new job and has helped dozens of people in this way. *SoFi* also offers personal loans, mortgages and wealth management.

Other US-based student loan firms worth checking out include *CommonBond*, *Earnest* and *Lendkey*. They each have a slightly different approach. *CommonBond* offers three different types of loans, a refinancing product to consolidate loans, one designed for parents of students and a product for MBA students. *Earnest* features a loan personalization tool called Precision Pricing, with the aim of helping students to prioritize debt and pay it off quickly. The focus on customizable repayment options makes it easy to increase minimum repayments or make multiple extra payments. *Lendkey* links student borrowers with loans from partner lenders in community banking and credit unions.

With so many options on offer in the United States, there is a definite need for a service to easily compare the various loan opportunities. *Credible* claims that students can save over US

$13,000 on average by using its comparison service to access multiple lenders. *Supermoney* offers a similar service.

Apps for that: *Future Finance, Prodigy Finance, Grant Fairy, SoFi, CommonBond, Earnest, Lendkey, Credible, Supermoney*

Notes

1 Peer to Peer Finance Association [accessed 12 December 2018] https://www.p2pfa.org.uk/news/
2 Transparency Market Research [accessed 30 June 2018] Peer to peer lending market [Online] www.transparencymarketresearch.com/pressrelease/peer-to-peer-lending-market.htm

Afterword

One of the biggest challenges in compiling this book has been that technology is changing all the time. New products, services and ideas are coming through at a daily rate. Every time I attend a fintech conference or judge a hackathon event, I see and hear about all the new things coming through and marvel at the energy and excitement that goes into making it all happen. Everyone involved seems to be spurred on by the widespread will to find better (and completely new) ways of doing things. It is what makes this such an exciting space to be in right now. Of course, not every idea succeeds. That's the nature of disruption. That shouldn't put innovators off trying though and it certainly does not. However, with new apps constantly arriving and some not making the grade, it does make it difficult to be completely up to date with a guide like this.

I have tried to take the changeable nature of this vibrant industry into account and hope you will bear with me if by the time you read this you find certain products have been super-seded by something that is even better. It's the price you pay for reading about new technology in a medium that is hundreds of years old. That said, the basics that I have outlined for each sector will hold true for some time to come. My advice would be to take the background material I have laid out about the various fintech developments and use it as a useful starting point. Don't be scared to explore this amazing fintech sector yourself either.

Blockchain and the future of (personal) finance

One technology that I have not spent too much time on here is *blockchain*. This is easily one of the most revolutionary technological changes on the horizon and may make a huge difference across the fintech sector. Indeed, if I were writing this book a few years from now, I would imagine that blockchain would play a far more dominant role in each and every chapter.

Blockchain underpins something called *cryptocurrency*. You may (unless you've been living in a cave since the mid-2010s) have heard of Bitcoin. You might even have noticed the term cryptocurrency popping up with increasing frequency. Yet, while most people have a vague idea that is it something to do with money and a lot of people seem to be getting very excited about it, in most cases that is probably as far as it goes.

It's early days in terms of the upside for you, the consumer. Unless you have particular requirements or interests that lead you to a direct interest in cryptocurrency, the areas that blockchain technologies will impact first may be in financial infrastructure or corporate finance, which are a bit out of view. But in my view, it is very much worth everyone's while to show an interest in the world of cryptocurrency. It may well play a big role in all of our financial futures.

Readers may not want to get deeply into the technology side of it and how it all works, and I fully appreciate that fact. However, it is helpful to set out a little bit of background to put things in context. A cryptocoin is a digital asset, something like cash that you own by having the ability to save it or spend it. Whereas cash is stored in a physical wallet, your ownership of a cryptocoin is really a matter of possessing the *secret key* needed to do anything with it. Managing these very long, cryptic keys is a bit difficult for humans so instead we store these coins in a digital wallet that takes care of things for us.

Blockchain refers to the technology underpinning all cryptocurrency transactions. Blockchains are public databases that anyone can look at, at any time. Think of blockchain as a sort of digital ledger, filled with blocks or digital pages that are a record of all the cryptocurrency purchases and transactions. You can inspect and explore Bitcoin's blockchain (the original blockchain) online at https://blockchain.info to get a better idea of how it works.

A block is just a chunk of transactions gathered together and wrapped up in such a way that they can be agreed on by everybody. The transactions that can be used to build a block are all broadcast and re-broadcast into the network continually until they end up in a block, and anyone can join the race to gather together a set of transactions into a block and add them to the end of the blockchain. This is called *mining* and by winning the race and mining a block you receive a financial reward from the network itself. (You may have heard the term 'mining Bitcoins'.) Whenever anyone uses cryptocurrency, spending or transferring it, their transaction is broadcast to the network as raw material for miners to construct new blocks in the blockchain. While many blockchains are entirely public (like Bitcoin's) the details of individual transactions are encrypted so you can't just browse the details of anyone's spending without possessing their secret keys.

If it helps to think of it in terms of traditional banking, imagine blockchain as an extensive history of banking transactions. Each Bitcoin transaction is entered chronologically, in just the same way as your ingoings and outgoings appear on your usual paper or online statements. Each block is like an individual bank statement that represents all the transactions in a short sequence of time (about 10 minutes for Bitcoin). Only it is a statement for everybody in the world, not just one account! Cryptocurrencies exist on many users' computers all over the world, rather than being stored in one central location.

You'll have noticed how important the miners are to this system. In exchange for validating transactions and building them into a blockchain, these miners receive a reward of cryptocurrency themselves. In fact, this is how all Bitcoin was created – it was all mined. This global race to place the next block on top of the blockchain and not get slowed down or sidetracked by invalid or copycat chains, is how we ensure that everybody agrees on the facts without any need for a centralized record-keeper. It also provides a degree of security and trust in the system because anyone wanting to cheat the system would have to work as hard and as quickly as all the other well-behaved participants put together. For Bitcoin, at the time of writing, that would famously require an electricity consumption equivalent to that of an entire country. (While I was writing this book, the Bitcoin network exceeded the electricity consumption of Ecuador and then Australia and is still growing.)

While Bitcoin is the best known cryptocurrency, partly because it was the first to appear and has therefore attracted significant investor and media attention since, there are now hundreds or thousands of variations on the theme, including Dash, Ether and Litecoin.

OK, you may be thinking, *that's an awful lot of techie stuff, with a whole lot of new names to understand, what has it got to do with me? How is it going to make me richer, or poorer?* I suspect that even if you have a passing curiosity about cryptocurrencies, the chances are you may well have been put off anything to do with the idea by lurid media warnings of a 'Bitcoin bubble', likening cryptocurrencies to the dotcom boom and bust of the late 1990s. Many news organizations have even taken the focus of the hysteria a few centuries back, warning that Bitcoin exposes us all to the risks presented by the Dutch tulip bulb mania. This was the feverish flower boom that hit its peak in 1637 when some single tulip bulbs were sold for more than 10 times the annual income of a skilled craftsperson, before the bulb market collapsed, taking with it the fortunes of various speculators. The media are not the only doomsayers. There have been many high profile figures who have predicted that Bitcoin and all the other cryptocurrencies will go the same way. Dire warnings have been issued about unrealistic pricing that will all collapse once enough of the 'get rich' crowd have jumped on the bandwagon and a tipping point is reached. There is no doubt the cryptocurrency markets have proven extremely volatile and treacherous for speculators.

While pictures of Bitcoin millionaires posing by their Lamborghinis always do make great media, a lot of the doom-laden coverage is rather missing the point. What many of these stories fail to acknowledge is that cryptocurrencies might actually have really important real-world applications. Cryptocurrencies like Bitcoin are both a payment system and money. It is the innovative *payment system* that is the real source of its value. Blockchain offers the ability to decentralize power from major organizations, which have dominated payment processes up until now and instead puts power into the hands of hundreds, even millions, of servers. You can theoretically make a payment to anybody in the world without a single bank or payment provider being involved in the transaction. Where, in switching from cash to cashless, we've placed many third parties in the chain between you and the shopkeeper, cryptocurrency might just take them back out of the chain again. The problem is, blockchain applications that make paying for rather mundane purchases such as mobile phone or electricity bills cheaper, more efficient and easier, are never going to hit the headlines while there are shiny sports cars to write about.

If you do begin to think about cryptocurrencies in a new way ie as a better, more efficient, safer, more private way of paying for things, rather than a speculative investment like buying shares or gold, they do have an appeal.

Cutting out the middlemen (and their fees)

It is still early days, as with so many things in fintech. Yet, there are already a number of notable advantages to digital currencies. For a start, they are in many ways more secure and reliable, which is always a good thing where money is concerned. (The frequent new stories about hacks at cryptocurrency exchanges more usually reflect on the practices of those exchanges than the underlying currency.) Any system that is less susceptible to fraud and can't be counterfeited benefits both sellers and buyers, as well as banks. There is less opportunity for identity theft too. If you pay by credit card, you give the merchant full access to your credit line, even if you are only spending a couple of pounds. This is because credit cards work on a *pull* basis, where the retailer initiates the payment and the amount is pulled from the customer's account. Cryptocurrencies work in the reverse way, *pushing* the money to the seller, so the exact amount is sent with no further information required or crucial personal details put at risk.

Perhaps most importantly, and the reason why so many fintechs are looking with such interest at cryptocurrencies, is they cut out the middlemen that pop up in so many transactions. And, as everyone knows, middlemen always come at a cost. Get rid of third-party intermediaries, which often charge high processing fees, and instead switch to direct payment between individuals, and the cost of transactions should come down markedly. It can make the whole payment process so much more transparent.

I should play devil's advocate here, because it is not all wine and roses in the cryptocurrencies and blockchain garden. There are some drawbacks. The biggest one is that very, very few people understand much about the new developments. (And if you've managed to get this far in this concluding section, you may be in agreement as to why. It is all quite new for many people and the surrounding technology does sound off-puttingly complex.) We are still a fair way away from the time when this technology is accepted by the masses. While the technology is available, there is no likelihood of cryptocurrencies replacing credit cards and traditional currencies in the near future. Most businesses, for example, don't accept them and, at the time of writing, very few appear to have any plans to do so until their use is a bit more widespread (which is a bit of a Catch 22, if you think about it).

Cryptocurrencies also have a bit of a reputation problem. The anonymity of the process has attracted members of the criminal fraternity, who are naturally quite keen that their transactions are kept private and never scrutinized too closely. This, in turn, has attracted the attention of governments and regulators who may yet decide it is all a giant money-laundering scheme and slap on some more stringent regulations that could have an impact on the value of these assets.

There are question marks too about just how far this can all be scaled up. The way Bitcoin is currently designed limits the speed and number of transactions that can be processed. For many cryptocurrencies, the performance of established payment networks like credit cards represents the gold standard of the performance they are aiming for and, despite many promising developments in flight, they are very far off that right now.

Blockchain technology is also being used in applications quite different from the original Bitcoin idea, to address issues such as digital identity, notarization, land registry and so forth, though there is little consensus yet about how successful these efforts will be.

As I say, it is early days, but it is certain that in one way or another, blockchain will play a big role in the next leap forward in multiple areas, including payment technology, which is why

I am noting it here. Watch this space, as I have said a few times in this book, which is, again, a reflection of just how dynamic this space can be.

No better time to make the most of your money

Other than cryptocurrencies, I see the future as being very much about the continuation of the unbundling of our traditional relationship with banking and finance. As I hope you have seen, the thread running through the book has been very much about changing the long-accepted arm's-length relationship we've had with financiers, where they told us what we needed (mostly because that was what they wanted to give us) and we had very little choice in the matter. Today, we are no longer bound to one large institution. The idea of having all your finances with one provider is as old fashioned as banking a cheque and waiting at least three days for it to be cashed. Many people are already using a range of different services for all of their various financial needs, and that situation is set to continue. Plus, thanks to open banking, this is being achieved in an ever more seamless way. The days of entering and re-entering your details and waiting patiently while your identity is checked once again are drawing to a close. One of the real beauties of the new crop of fintech apps is you barely need to think twice about how they all work. Just enjoy that they *do* work and that access to (and knowledge about) your cash is so much more readily available. Then all you need to do is reap the benefits of a more organized, fairer, transparent financial system.

Whatever happens, technology will continue to completely redefine how we use money and run our financial lives. We truly are in the midst of a money revolution. Fintech disruptors are tackling everything to do with our money and financial obligations, across a range of sectors from savings, to health, to education, to business. Nothing has been left out. New solutions are coming on board every day, offering advice 24/7, all of which go towards helping everyone save and spend their money more efficiently. Plus, of course, it is so much easier to pay for things thanks to the explosion in online payment apps that integrate with our bank accounts.

Mobility has played a huge role in these developments. The ubiquitous smartphone has paved the way for our seamless interaction with bank and financial services apps anywhere and everywhere, giving us all smart real-time insights into our cash situation at any time of the day or night. This is also not to forget the extraordinary potential for the estimated 2 billion people in the world who are completely unbanked. Thanks to mobile phones people with no bank account will, for the first time ever, have access to financial services. There really has never been a better time when it comes to making well-informed decisions about your money.

Since I come from a background of what is often called traditional banking, I am more aware than most people of just how far we have come in an astonishingly short space of time. We have moved from a situation where the so-called establishment were perceived to be the only organizations that could be trusted to protect what is most dear to people, to one where consumers are relishing the opportunities brought to them through a greater choice. Fintechs have already pioneered a long list of firsts that have changed the game for the financial industry. There are now chatbots for customer service that use machine learning to continuously update their knowledge by following our interactions, AI for fraud protection, biometrics for stronger account security, and blockchain begins to promise faster, cheaper ways to transact. Many of the services in use today bypass the need for human interaction, saving the customer time and money, while also ensuring the best possible rates. Interestingly, many established banks and financial services institutions are now trying to replicate what the more fleet of foot fintechs are achieving. But look closely though, and you'll see that is where the similarities end. Underneath the rush to keep up and modernize, these established businesses remain the same, since they are built on outmoded technology and practices. This is why they still charge hefty fees (the details of which may well be artfully buried in the small print) and move at a painfully slow pace.

One of the biggest differences between fintechs and their forebears is the new kids on the block are fixated on a customer-first approach. Fintechs are focussed on building fairer financial models, with better features and functionality. As start-ups beginning from scratch and looking to disrupt an established industry, they have the advantage of low overheads. This means a better deal for customers and the benefit of the very latest technology framework to back up the innovations. Machine learning is being used to build products that actively work with you to make sure you don't get into financial trouble. Meanwhile, evolving AI continually looks out for your future well-being, so you have enough for unexpected bills, or in your pension pot, or to pay for big financial goals.

If it all sounds a little overwhelming, remember there is no compulsion to adopt everything that has been detailed in this book all at once. The apps I have described are a broad illustration of what is out there, which I hope will help you to make an informed choice. Use the information as a reference and connect with products as and when you need them, whether it be a loan, cash for your travels or a better deal on your car insurance.

By my estimation, using just some of the products and services detailed here could save you hundreds of pounds a year. Improvements to the visibility of your finances have an even bigger potential to make you better off. You'll also save time, since you won't have to constantly hunt around for the best deals, because all that will be done for you by your very own pocket digital bank manager. This is a brilliant opportunity for everyone to create a more open and a healthier relationship with money, which can only ever be a good thing.

We are at the beginning of a revolution in the way we save, spend and manage our cash. Let's make the most of it.

Index